Journeys Three
Religious Education
for Key Stage 3 Northern Ireland

Francine ~~Gilson~~
and Fra~~nces~~ Boyd

HODDER
EDUCATION
AN HACHETTE UK COMPANY

The Publishers would like to thank the following for permission to reproduce copyright material:

Photo credits

p.6 © Alexander Raths/iStockphoto.com; **p.12** © Image State Media; **p.15** *L–R* © deanm1974/Fotolia; © Michelle Robek/Fotolia; © Monkey Business/Fotolia; © Adam Borkowski/Fotolia; © Stockbyte/Getty Images; © Monkey Business/Fotolia; © Monkey Business/Fotolia; © corepics/Fotolia; © Liv Friis-Larsen/Fotolia; © Christian J. Stewart/iStockphoto.com; © Kirsty Pargeter/Fotolia; © iQoncept/Fotolia; **p.17** *Top right clockwise* © Ingram Publishing Limited; © 1997 Jules Frazier/Photodisc/Getty Images; © Oleg Kozlov/Fotolia; © Stockbyte/Getty Images; © Scott T. Baxter/Photodisc/Getty Images; © iStockphoto.com; © 1997 Doug Menuez/Photodisc/Getty Images; **p.20** © Matt Meadows/Peter Arnold Inc./Science Photo; **p.21** *Top* © Angela Hampton Picture Library/ Alamy; *Bottom* © Christa Brunt/iStockphoto.com; **p.22** *Top* © Roger Bamber/Alamy; *Top left clockwise* © Ingram Publishing Limited; © Ingram Publishing Limited; © Ingram Publishing Limited; © David H. Lewis/iStockphoto.com; © iStockphoto.com; © Ingram Publishing Limited; **p.25** © catcha/Fotolia; **p.26** © Bananastock/Photolibrary Group Ltd; **p.28** © www.learningfundamentals.com.au; **p.29** *L–R* © World History Archive/Alamy; © Mary Evans Picture Library/Alamy; © Classic Image/Alamy; © Sipa Press/Rex Features; © Classic Image/Alamy; **p.30** *L–R* © Mary Evans Picture Library/Alamy; © Lordprice Collection/Alamy; **p.31** © World History Archive/Alamy; **p.32** *Top– bottom* © Classic Image/Alamy; © North Wind Picture Archives/Alamy; © Martin Shields/Alamy; **p.34** © Classic Image/Alamy; **p.35** *L–R* © Dan Vincent/Alamy; © Kaiser/Alamy; **p.36** *Top* © Amy Katherine Dragoo/Alamy; *Bottom* © Mary Evans Picture Library/Alamy; **p.39** *Top* © CSU Archives/Everett Collection/Rex Features; *Bottom* © Everett Collection/Rex Features; **p.40** © Sipa Press/Rex Features; **p.43** © Robert Harding Picture Library Ltd/ Alamy; **p.45** © Nabil Biyahmadine; **p.47** © C. Lee/PhotoLink/Photodisc/Getty Images; **p.48** © Julien Grondin/ iStockphoto.com; **p.49** *Top–bottom* © Stockbyte/Photolibrary Group Ltd; © Simon Price/Alamy; © Stockbyte/ Photolibrary Group Ltd; **p.50** *L–R* © Pontino/Alamy; © Alex Motrenko/Fotolia; © Mele Avery/Fotolia; **p.55** © Ian West/PA Archive/Press Association Images; **p.57** *Pictures 1, from top clockwise* © ni press photos/Alamy; © John Eccles/ Alamy; © Simon Stacpoole/Rex Features; *Pictures 2, from top clockwise* © 1997 John A. Rizzo/Photodisc/Getty Images; © 1995 C.Borland/PhotoLink/Photodisc/Getty Images; © Bananastock/Photolibrary Group Ltd; **p.58** *L–R* © Christopher Pillitz/Alamy; © Elizabeth Leyden/Alamy; **p.59** © Jan Sochor/Alamy; **p.61** © Rex Features; **p.62** © Eye Ubiquitous/Alamy; **p.67** © Jon Arnold Images Ltd/Alamy; **p.75** © Craig Lovell/Eagle Visions Photography/Alamy; **p.80** © Roger Cracknell 09/UK/Alamy; **p.81** © Photodisc/Getty Images; **p.82** © Asia/Alamy

Acknowledgements

p.19 Logo reproduced with permission of the Pioneer Total Abstinence Association; **p.41** Salvadorean painted crucifix courtesy of Central American Crafts, Cape Clear Island; **p.53** Photo courtesy of Fr Declan O'Loughlan; **p.61** Reuters news article reproduced with permission of PARS International; **p.64** Logo reproduced with permission of The Corrymeela Community, www.corrymeela.org; **p.79** Photo of Buddhist shrine courtesy of Potala Buddhist Centre, Belfast; **p.83** Photo of Buddhist café courtesy of Potala Buddhist Centre, Belfast

Every effort has been made to trace all copyright holders, but if any have been inadvertently overlooked the Publishers will be pleased to make the necessary arrangements at the first opportunity.

Although every effort has been made to ensure that website addresses are correct at time of going to press, Hodder Education cannot be held responsible for the content of any website mentioned in this book. It is sometimes possible to find a relocated web page by typing in the address of the home page for a website in the URL window of your browser.

Hachette UK's policy is to use papers that are natural, renewable and recyclable products and made from wood grown in sustainable forests. The logging and manufacturing processes are expected to conform to the environmental regulations of the country of origin.

Orders: please contact Bookpoint Ltd, 130 Milton Park, Abingdon, Oxon OX14 4SB. Telephone: (44) 01235 827720. Fax: (44) 01235 400454. Lines are open 9.00–5.00, Monday to Saturday, with a 24-hour message answering service. Visit our website at www.hoddereducation.co.uk

© Francine Magill, Linda Colson and Frances Boyd 2010
First published in 2010 by
Hodder Education,
An Hachette UK Company
338 Euston Road
London NW1 3BH

Impression number   5 4 3 2 1

Year   2014 2013 2012 2011 2010

Cover photo © Sindre Ellingsen/Photographers Choice/Getty Images
Illustrations by Alex Machin and GreenGate Publishing Services
Typeset in Minion 11pt by GreenGate Publishing Services, Tonbridge, Kent
Printed in Italy

A catalogue record for this title is available from the British Library

ISBN: 978 0340 969 717

Contents

Preface
About this book

In Chapters 1–6 you will find:

▶ **Learning intentions**. These tell you the skills and knowledge you will be learning in the chapter.

▶ **Skills and capabilities icons**. These show you at a glance where you have the opportunity to develop some cross-curricular skills. These icons are explained in the table below.

▶ **Get Active**. These are tasks which help you improve your thinking and practise your skills in Religious Education.

▶ **The big task**. This helps you pull together all your work at the end of the chapter and gives you the opportunity to reflect on your own performance.

▶ **Key words**. Bold terms are defined in a glossary at the back of the book.

Skill/Capability	Icon	Description
Managing information		Research and manage information effectively to investigate religious, moral and ethical issues, including using mathematics and using ICT where appropriate.
Thinking, problem solving, decision making		Show deeper understanding by thinking critically and flexibly, solving problems and making informed decisions.
Being creative		Demonstrate creativity and initiative when developing ideas and following them through.
Working with others		Work effectively with others.
Self-management		Demonstrate self-management by working systematically, persisting with tasks, evaluating and improving own performance.

Key elements

Throughout your Key Stage 3 Religious Education course you will also study ideas and concepts which help develop your understanding of the key elements of the curriculum, as shown in the table below.

Key element	Description
Personal understanding	Explore how religion has affected your personal identity, culture and lifestyle.
Mutual understanding	Investigate how religion has been selectively interpreted to create stereotypical perceptions and to justify views and actions.
Personal health	Investigate connections between religion and perceptions of personal health.
Moral character	Investigate individuals who are considered to have taken a significant moral stand and examine their motivation and legacy.
Spiritual awareness	Investigate and evaluate the spiritual beliefs and legacies of different religions.
Citizenship	Investigate how religion affects our contributions to society.
Cultural understanding	Investigate how religion affects our understanding of other cultures and other groups in our own culture.
Media awareness	Critically investigate and evaluate the impact of the media on religious belief.
Ethical awareness	Investigate ethical issues in religion or key figures who have behaved ethically or unethically.
Employability	Investigate how the skills developed through religious study will be useful in a range of careers, and consider careers associated with religious practice.
Economic awareness	Investigate the changing relation between religion and economic solvency.
Education for sustainable development	Investigate the active role that religion can play in the local and global environment.

Introduction

It's hard to believe that you are now in Year Ten. It seems like no time at all since you were setting out on your Year Eight journey. We hope that you've enjoyed the first two books and that the approaches your teachers have been using have made your learning in RE both fun and interesting. As you get older the questions you ask will become deeper, more wide-ranging and perhaps more challenging. We hope that you will find the material in *Journeys Three* relevant, stimulating and engaging and that as a result of many active learning experiences you will want to find out more about the exciting, interesting and often controversial area that we call religion.

As in *Journeys One* and *Two* we want to help you develop skills: in communication, in using ICT and even sometimes, in using mathematics! We want to help you to learn to manage information, to think, to solve problems and to make informed decisions. We want to encourage you to be creative, to manage your own work effectively and to work well with others.

We hope that through using the *Assessment for Learning* process you will be able to take greater responsibility for your own learning in RE, taking stock of where you currently are and moving on from there. We also offer opportunities for you to learn not just how to assess your own learning but to recognise what 'good' looks like in your friends' work as well.

Hopefully *Journeys Three* will encourage you to think about what it means to show concern and respect for others, to take personal responsibility for your actions and to show integrity, moral courage, commitment and determination. Perhaps most importantly of all though, we hope that you will begin to develop not just an inner appreciation of life's purpose, but also personal strengths and resources that will help you cope with challenges and difficulties that life sometimes throws in our direction.

Have a good year!

Chapter 1 Right or wrong!

Learning intentions

I am learning:

▶ to explore how people form their own moral values

▶ to explore and discuss different views that people have about what is right and what is wrong

▶ to consider religious views on right and wrong

▶ to identify issues in our society and consider differing opinions on these issues.

a) Violence is always wrong. People should never use violence.

b) Trespassing on other people's property is wrong.

c) Lying is always wrong.

d) It's ok to steal if it is necessary to stay alive.

Discuss

1 Discuss the statements in the speech bubbles above and decide as a group if you think they are true or false.
2 Discuss your decision with the class.

1.1 Where do we get our morals from?

Throughout our lives we often have to make difficult decisions. Knowing what is the right thing to do can be hard. From an early age we are taught the difference between right and wrong. If, as children, we did something that our parents thought was wrong or dangerous we would have been reprimanded and told not to do it again. Sometimes we learn from an experience that something will hurt us and that it is the WRONG thing to do. We also learn that we have done the RIGHT thing because something has turned out well or if we have been praised for what we did.

Our questions in this chapter are about **MORALS**.

▶ What are morals?

▶ Where do we learn our own **MORAL VALUES**?

A dictionary definition of the word moral is:

> **Moral** *adj.* concerned with right and wrong conduct; based on a sense of right and wrong.

Doing wrong

Doing right

Get Active 1

1 Working in groups think about where and how we learn the difference between RIGHT and WRONG. Copy and complete the spider diagram on the right in your notebook. Write down as many different examples as you can.

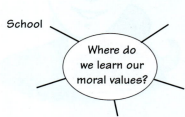

School

Where do we learn our moral values?

2 Individually rank your top five answers by writing the numbers 1–5 on your spider diagram (1 = top answer).

3 Write down your top answer. Underneath explain why you think this is the most important answer.

4 Share your answer with the rest of the class.

In our society, throughout our lives, we are often faced with what are called 'Moral Dilemmas'. This is when we have to make a decision to do something. There may be a number of different options that we could choose. Sometimes it is hard to know exactly what to do. At this time people would say that they are often guided by the moral values that they have been taught throughout their lives. These moral values can come from a number of different people or groups in our lives (for example, family, school, religion etc.). We choose to do something because we believe it is the right action to take.

Get Active 2

1 Read the following story:

> John had been saving up his pay from his part-time job for something special. He wanted to buy a new computer game console – the latest on the market. He had a console but this new one was even better. For weeks now he had not spent any of his pay because he wanted to have the console before the school holidays started. His mum had promised to buy him some games if he did well in his exams.
>
> In Citizenship classes at school John had been learning about charity work. They had been looking at one particular charity that helped people across the world who lived in poverty. John had written a project and had found out all about their work and how much it cost to help people. In his evaluation he wrote that more people should be willing to give money to the charity. He got a really good mark for his project – especially his evaluation. His teacher asked him if he gave money to the charity. This made John think about his savings as he really wanted to help. He began to wonder if he needed a new game console after all …

2 Decide what you think John should do with his savings – what is the RIGHT thing to do? Write this down in your notebook.

3 Give two reasons why you think this is the RIGHT thing to do.

4 Discuss your decision with your partner. Comment on your partner's decision.

1.2 What do religions teach us?

Many of the laws and rules that govern our society were developed in line with Christian religious values. Northern Ireland has traditionally been seen as a Christian country and many of the laws that we have are based on biblical rules such as the Ten Commandments. The influence of religion may have recently declined, with fewer people attending church on a regular basis, but the moral values that Christianity teaches are still important to many people.

The Ten Commandments are seen by Christians and Jews as important rules given to human beings by God. They can be divided into two categories:

▶ Rules about how to act before God

▶ Rules about how to treat other people.

The Ten Commandments were written on a stone tablet

Get Active 1

1 The table below summarises the Ten Commandments. Copy it into your notebook.

A summary of the Ten Commandments	
1 Have no other gods but me.	6 Don't kill anyone.
2 Do not make idols to worship.	7 Be faithful to your husband or wife.
3 You must not use God's name badly.	8 Do not steal.
4 Remember to keep the Sabbath holy – do not work. Keep the day to worship God.	9 Do not tell lies about people.
5 Respect your parents.	10 Do not be jealous of the things that other people have.

2 Highlight the rules that relate to how we should act before God in YELLOW. Highlight the rules that relate to how we should act towards others in PINK.

3 Discuss the commandments with your partner using the following questions:

▶ Do you think all the commandments are relevant to our society today? If not all of them, which commandments are still relevant and why?

▶ Do you think some of the commandments are more important than others? If yes, make a list of the commandments you think are the most important.

▶ Do you think these commandments would influence people in making decisions about right and wrong?

4 Share your main discussion points with the class.

Many religions around the world share similar moral values, especially in rules about how humans should treat each other. Members of each world religion are guided by the rules set down within their faith.

In Islam, the idea of community is very important. Muslims are taught that they should care for one another as they would care for a family member.

In Buddhism (see chapter 6) the **Noble Eightfold Path** guides Buddhists in their everyday lives.

Get Active 2

1   Read the summary of some of the guidelines in the Eightfold Path below.

Right understanding – You should understand the Four Noble Truths (these are the important teachings in Buddhism).

Right thought – You must think about the kind of life you lead and decide to live in a caring and unselfish way.

Right speech – Always speak in ways that are kind, truthful and not hurtful to yourself or other people.

Right action – Behave in ways that respect living things, respect other people's property, respect other people's feelings and respect yourself.

Right livelihood – Do a job that does not lead to harming others.

Right effort – Do your best to avoid bad things and do good things.

Right self-awareness – Control of your mind is important. Be aware of your own thoughts and the world around you.

Right meditation – Meditation is important. It helps people to concentrate and to follow the other rules.

2   Use the information you have about the Ten Commandments and the Eightfold Path to complete the following table in your notebook:

Similarities between the Ten Commandments and the Eightfold Path	Differences between the Ten Commandments and the Eightfold Path

1.3 All you need is love

Joseph Fletcher was an Anglican Minister who was interested in how people make decisions and respond to moral dilemmas.

He claimed that there are three ways of making a moral decision:

1   Every decision is governed by rules/laws. Laws are developed from religion, or from people's experience. These are then followed in every situation without exception, for example, the Ten Commandments.

2   Every decision is approached as if it is completely new and has never happened before. Every decision made is unique.

The third way is something that Joseph Fletcher called 'Situation ethics'. He saw this as a compromise between the other two.

3   Every decision in a situation is made with one thing in mind, LOVE/COMPASSION.

Joseph Fletcher used the example of Jesus and his attitude to the Jewish law to explain his theory. Jesus often got into trouble with the Pharisees (the Jewish leaders) because his teaching did not always follow the rules they had developed. One story in the Bible tells us about Jesus healing a woman on the Sabbath (Jewish day of rest). The Pharisees accused him of working on the Sabbath because he had healed someone.

This is what Jesus said:

Showing compassion to the elderly

> You hypocrites! Doesn't each of you on the Sabbath untie his donkey from the stall and lead it out to give it water? Then should not this woman, who has been sick for eighteen years, be freed from her illness?

The Pharisees had taken the Ten Commandments and other rules from the Torah (Old Testament) and added to them so that there were rules for every possible situation in life. Jesus went back to the first principles of the law: LOVE.

Get Active 1

1   Read the full story of Jesus healing the woman in Luke 13: 10–17.

2   Answer the following questions in your notebook:

    a   Why were the Pharisees so annoyed with Jesus?

    b   How did Jesus explain his actions?

    c   Do you think that Jesus was right to break the law about the Sabbath? Explain your answer.

Get Active 2

1 Look up the following verses from the Bible and write down in your notebook what they say about love:

  ▶ Luke 10: 27

  ▶ John 15: 13

  ▶ 1 John 3: 23

2 Discuss with your partner the information on page 6 and the Bible passages. Do you think that the Beatles were right when they sang the song 'All you need is love'?

3 Can you and your partner think of a situation where the principle of love might mean going against a law/rule that you think is important (for example, telling a lie to protect someone in danger)? Discuss this with the rest of the class.

For Fletcher the **principle of love** can be applied to every situation and will help humans to achieve the greatest good.

He made six proposals to help people follow the **love ethic:**

1 Only one thing is basically good. That one thing is LOVE.

2 People should make decisions following the rule of love and nothing else.

3 If you follow the rule of love then you will be doing the right thing (justice).

4 Love means that we will want what is best for everyone whether we like them or not.

5 Only the end (the result) justifies the means.

6 Decisions based on love are made according to the situation/moral dilemma that someone is in.

Joseph Fletcher stated that the commandment on the right is the one that people should follow in all situations.

LUKE 10: 27
Love the Lord your God with all your heart and with all your soul and with all your strength and with all your mind, and love your neighbour as yourself.

Get Active 3

1 Individually write down any questions that you have about the six proposals to help people follow the love ethic.

2 Working in groups, discuss each other's questions and on poster paper make a list of questions that your group has about these proposals. Rank your questions from 1–5 (1 = most important).

3 As a class, discuss the most important questions that you have. Decide on the class's top five questions and write them on a large sheet of paper.

4 Write down any answers that you have to the questions on another sheet of paper.

5 Display the questions and answers on a display board under the heading 'All you need is love'.

1.4 Lying

Get Active 1

1   Read the two scenarios below and discuss with your partner what you would do and why:

Scenario 1
Your mum has just come home from the hairdressers and you dislike her new hairstyle. What do you say when she asks what you think?

Scenario 2
Your friend loves to sing but doesn't seem to realise that she can't sing very well. The school holds auditions for a musical and your friend is really disappointed when she doesn't get a part. She asks you why you think she didn't get a part. What do you say?

2   Discuss your responses with the class. Did anyone within the class choose to lie? If so why?

Is lying always wrong?

The six major world faiths all condemn lying, yet it is in all likelihood something that all of us do. Why is that? Why do nearly all of us lie even when we know it is wrong?

The question 'Is lying always wrong?' has been debated for centuries. Most of us can think of situations where telling the truth would cause someone pain, insult them or even damage the relationship you have with them. However, does this make it right to lie? How might a person feel if they discovered that they had been lied to?

Think …
What would you consider wrong to lie about?

What would you consider acceptable to lie about?

There are many different answers to the question 'Is lying always wrong?'. At one end of the spectrum is Immanuel Kant (1724–1804) who believed that all lying was wrong regardless of the circumstances. St. Augustine (354–430), a Christian **theologian**, also taught that all lying was wrong but realised that this was very difficult to live up to. He believed that some lies could be forgiven and on rare occasions lying would be the right thing to do. He categorised lies into eight types, with the most difficult to forgive at the top and the easiest to forgive at the bottom.

▶ lies when teaching religion

▶ lies that hurt someone but help no one

▶ lies that hurt people but benefit another person

▶ lies for the fun of lying to someone

▶ lies during conversation to make others happy

▶ lies that help someone and hurt no one

▶ lies that hurt no one but help a person to find forgiveness from God

▶ lies that hurt no one but protect a person from being harmed.

At the other end of the spectrum is **utilitarianism**. John Stuart Mill (1806–1873) believed that a decision should be based on what would make the most people happy. Therefore if a lie would make more people happy than telling the truth, telling a lie is a better choice.

Get Active 2

1 Which of the three philosophers would you agree with about when lying is wrong and why: Immanuel Kant, St. Augustine or John Stuart Mill?

2 Look back at the two scenarios in Get Active 1. What difficulties might a person encounter if they chose to make their decisions based on:

   a Kant

   b Augustine

   c Mill?

3 Why do people choose to lie? Write down as many reasons as you can.

4 A Christian believes that it is wrong to lie as it is one of the Ten Commandments. Which philosopher do you think they would agree with and why?

1.5 Just war

The 'just war' theory sets out guidelines that a country can follow in order to ensure that any military action taken against another country is conducted within a legal and moral framework. There are two sets of criteria that must be fulfilled in order to make a war 'just'.

▶ *Jus ad bellum* – the right to go to war.

▶ *Jus in bello* – the right conduct while fighting a war.

Both criteria must be met to make the war just. Although a country may have gone to war for the right reasons, if the war is fought immorally it is no longer considered a just war.

Jus ad bellum

A country that wishes to go to war must show that its cause is justifiable. A modern definition of a just cause was defined by the US Catholic Conference in 1993. It stated:

> *'Force may be used only to correct a grave, public evil,*
> *that is, aggression or massive violation of the basic*
> *human rights of whole populations.'*

Jus in bello

How a war is conducted is very important. An intended attack must always be to help defeat the enemy. The bombing of civilian residential areas is prohibited unless a military target is within the vicinity. However, if it is quite clear that the loss of civilian lives outweighs the military advantage gained then attack on this target is also prohibited. This principle should be considered when any military attack is planned. This is to limit severe and needless death and devastation.

Jus post bellum

This third criterion has been added in recent years. It is concerned with justice after a war. It includes reconstruction, war crime trials, peace treaties and war reparations.

Think …

Why do you think wars are fought?

What are the reasons behind going to war?

Are any of these reasons justifiable?

Get Active 1

Select a search engine and type in the following address:

www.bbc.co.uk/ethics/war/just/against.shtml

Listed on this page are some arguments against the just war theory. Carefully read through each of the arguments. Which of the arguments do you agree with most and why? Which do you disagree with most and why?

Where did the 'just war' theory come from?

The 'just war' theory first originated with classical philosophers in Greece and Rome before the birth of Christ. The Church that began after Christ's death was pacifist (against any sort of violence and war). Origen, an early Church leader, said that Christians 'do not go forth as soldiers'. However, this attitude changed when the Roman Empire adopted Christianity as the state religion. The Council of Arles in 314 CE said to deny 'the state the right to go to war was to condemn it to extinction'. It was then that the Church began to devise its own 'just war' theory.

Christianity and war

In Christianity today there are differing points of view about war. Many would agree that war is hardly ever justified and should only happen if the 'just war' guidelines are followed. These Christians believe that at times war is the lesser of two evils. Others are pacifists and would refuse to take part in any war. One such Christian group is the Quakers who are totally committed to non-violence.

Get Active 2

Copy and complete the table on the right. Write down the name of at least five wars in the war column. Place a tick in either the just or unjust column depending on whether you think the 'just war' principles were followed. Write down your reason.

War	Just	Reason	Unjust	Reason

1.6 Saviour siblings

What are saviour siblings?

A **saviour sibling** is a baby who has been created to save the life of a brother or sister who is suffering from a very serious illness. Usually the sick child will have a form of anaemia that will eventually lead to his or her death if not treated. The only form of treatment for this type of anaemia is a bone marrow transplant or stem cell infusion.

What are stem cells?

Stem cells are cells that can turn into any kind of cell. Your body is full of different types of cells – cells that make up your muscles, nails, hair, skin, etc. All of these cells originally came from stem cells.

Should a baby be created to save the life of another?

What is stem cell infusion?

Stem cell infusion is when healthy compatible stem cells are transplanted into the diseased part of the body to replace the damaged ones. These then grow and form into the necessary cells that allow the body to function properly.

Where do stem cells come from?

There are various places that stem cells can be harvested from:

▶ Embryonic stem cells – these are taken from an **embryo** seven to ten days after fertilisation.

▶ Foetal stem cells – these are taken from aborted **fetuses**.

▶ Umbilical cord stem cells – umbilical cord blood contains stem cells similar to those found in bone marrow.

▶ Placenta stem cells – these are taken from a **placenta**.

▶ Adult stem cells – many adult tissues contain stem cells that can be isolated.

A saviour sibling is a baby that has been **genetically engineered** to have stem cells or bone marrow that is compatible with their sibling.

How is this done?

DNA technology has advanced to allow technicians to review embryos that have been fertilised in a laboratory to discover if one is a suitable match to the sibling. This is called Pre-Implantation Genetic Diagnosis (PGD). Once a suitable embryo has been found it is implanted into the mother's womb. After the baby is born stem cells are harvested from its umbilical cord.

What do Christians believe about saviour siblings?

There are many different opinions about saviour siblings and stem cell research and some are outlined here. Many Christians believe that a human life begins as soon as the sperm fertilises the egg. Subsequently they state that the embryo should be given the same respect as a child or adult. Therefore they would consider it wrong to dispose of an embryo merely because it is not compatible with the sibling.

Others believe that it is wrong to create a child to save another. They believe that a baby should be wanted for itself and not because of what he or she can do for another person. Some Christians say that we should accept the children that God gives us as gifts and not create children with specific characteristics to satisfy a need.

Some Christians believe that to create a saviour sibling is a loving and compassionate act. Jesus healed the sick and saving a life is good. The baby is not being harmed in any way.

Get Active 1

1   Read the scenario below and discuss:

> You are the parent of a baby who has the form of anaemia that needs a bone marrow transplant or stem cell infusion in order to live. No one in the family has suitable bone marrow and when you enquire about a donor on the bone marrow register there is no one compatible. In order to try and save the life of your child you decide to have a saviour sibling.

2   What issues do you need to think about before committing to this course of action and why?

Get Active 2

> Christians believe that Jesus healed people and showed compassion for those who were sick. Christians want to follow Jesus' example and help those who are ill.

1   Do you think stem cell technology is following Jesus' example by showing compassion and healing people, or do you think it is wrong? Explain your answer.

2   Imagine you are a child who was born to save a sibling. Write a diary account about the day your parents told you why you were born. Include all your thoughts and emotions about how you feel and why you feel like this.

Summary

▶ Moral values are the values that we learn throughout our lives that help us to make important decisions.

▶ Moral values can come from our upbringing, our religious beliefs or society.

▶ There are many difficult situations that people find themselves in during their lifetimes and people make decisions on what to do based on their own moral values.

Right or wrong!: the big task

Now you have completed this chapter on 'Right or wrong', do the following task:

1 Split into groups of six.

2 As a group, put together a twelve-page magazine with articles about moral values and consequences. This magazine is directed at teenagers. Each person in the group is responsible for one double-page spread within the magazine (two pages).

3 As a class discuss with your teacher the success criteria for the piece and ensure that these are displayed at all times.

4 As a group decide on a name for your magazine and how you are going to work together to complete the task.

5 After completing the task, peer assess the work of the other groups, giving two positive comments and one comment for improvement.

Chapter 2
Lifestyle choices

Learning intentions

I am learning:

▶ to define what addiction is

▶ to understand the problems drunkenness can cause within the family and discover Christian attitudes towards alcohol

▶ to explore the damage smoking can do to the individual

▶ to research the dangers of taking illegal drugs

▶ to examine why it is important to work and to use your spare time wisely

▶ to appreciate the money that I have and discuss Christian attitudes towards money.

Discuss

The collage above shows many different lifestyle choices. Decide with your partner which are good lifestyle choices and which are bad. Discuss how a middle-aged person would look if they had made good lifestyle choices throughout their life, and why they would look like this. Draw a cartoon of them and write an explanation. Then discuss how a middle-aged person would look if they had made bad lifestyle choices throughout their life, and why they would look like this. Your partner should draw a cartoon of them and write an explanation.

2.1 Making a choice

Discuss

Look at the picture on the right and read the text inside it.

What do you think this means and how might it influence the lifestyle choices that a Christian makes?

Do you not know that your body is a temple of the Holy Spirit, which is in you, and you have received from God?

Christians believe that God has given each of us the responsibility to look after our bodies because they are special. How we treat our bodies affects not only our body but also our mind and spirit. Christians therefore believe that as individuals we need to be very careful about what we eat, drink and put into our body.

Regardless of whether someone is a Christian or not, they only have one body, which should be respected in order for it to last as long as possible.

Get Active 1

1 In groups and on poster paper, draw an outline of a body like the illustration above.
2 Write around the body different ways people may abuse it.
3 Beside each example write down how this abuse affects the body.
4 Look at your list and, with a red colouring pencil, shade in any examples of abuse that you think might affect the mind.
5 With a green colouring pencil shade in any examples of abuse that you think might affect the spirit.
6 Decide which abuse causes the most damage to a person and place a number one beside it. Write an explanation for your choice.
7 Each group should explain their diagram to the class.

There are many ways a person can abuse their body. For example, overeating, not eating enough, insufficient exercise, excessive exercising, drinking too much tea, coffee, caffeinated energy drinks or alcohol, smoking, taking drugs and substance abuse – the list could go on and at times it seems difficult to strike the right balance and live a healthy lifestyle. Despite this, many young people are eager and successful in keeping themselves fit and healthy. However, there are some young people who make lifestyle choices that are harmful to their body, mind and spirit.

Addiction

Some lifestyle choices can lead people to become **addicted** to things that will cause physical and mental illness, financial ruin and death. Many of these things not only harm the individual but because of the effect they have on them, it causes heartache and pain to their family as well.

What is addiction?

The Chambers dictionary defines an addict as:

> **Addict** *v.* & *n.* someone who is dependent on something, often on a drug or alcohol, either physically or mentally.
>
> **Addictive** *adj.* creating dependence, habit forming.

What do addicts look like?

Very often we have an idea in our heads of what someone with an addition looks like. Identify from the pictures on the right which one you think represents your perception of someone with an addiction. Discuss with a partner the person you have chosen and explain your choice.

Any of the people in these pictures could have an addiction. Addicts come in all shapes and sizes, across age ranges, gender and social standing. Therefore it is not easy to spot an addict, and even close friends and family may not know someone has an addiction until it becomes impossible to hide it.

Get Active 2

1 Working in groups, read through a newspaper to find an article that relates to an addictive substance. For example, drunk driving.

2 Cut out the article and stick it into the middle of a piece of A3 paper.

3 Think about who has been affected by the addicts use of the substance and how this may have affected them. Write these ideas around the article.

2.2 Alcohol

Alcohol is an addictive substance and can cause individuals, families and communities many problems. However, when it is consumed within the recommended guidelines, it can be enjoyed without causing any damage.

Alcohol becomes a problem when a person drinks too much. Drinking too much leads to drunkenness when people have less control over their actions and responses. An excessive drinking habit can lead to damaged internal organs.

Drunkenness has been a problem from the first time humans discovered how to make alcohol. One of the problems with being drunk is that someone may not be fully in control of what they are doing or saying. The first story of someone being drunk in the Bible can be found in the very first book, Genesis. Noah had planted a vineyard, made some wine and drank too much of it. This led to all sorts of trouble both for himself and his family. Alcohol can cause problems not only for the individual but for their family and community.

Christian attitudes towards alcohol

For the first 1800 years of church history, Christians drank alcohol as a part of everyday life. It was believed that alcohol was a gift from God and to be enjoyed. However, they did teach that drunkenness was a sin.

This attitude towards alcohol changed in the nineteenth century when many Christians were concerned about the destructive influence alcohol was having on people's lives, particularly the poor. It was not unknown for poorer people to spend a significant portion of their income on alcohol, often leaving their children with little or no food. Some men were also physically abusive towards their wives when under the influence of alcohol. It was during this time that the '**temperance movement**' began. Initially the movement encouraged people to sign a pledge stating they would never drink spirits again, but they could drink wine and beer. Over time the pledge changed to declare that a person would not drink any alcohol again and some pledges even stated that the person would not provide alcohol to another person.

Get Active 1

Look back at the collage of people on the previous page. In pairs think of a reason why each of the people may want to get drunk. Discuss these reasons with the class.

The attitude Christians have towards alcohol today varies. All Christians believe that becoming drunk is wrong as the Bible states:

> **EPHESIANS 5: 18**
> *Do not get drunk with wine. That will ruin you spiritually. Instead be filled with the spirit.*

However, while some churches believe that no alcohol should be consumed, others believe that alcohol in moderation is fine. Some Protestant churches have replaced the communion wine with non-alcoholic red grape juice to ensure that if there is an alcoholic in the church that day they are not tempted. Although the Roman Catholic Church teaches that alcohol in moderation is fine there is a group within Ireland called the 'Pioneer Total Abstinence Association'. This grew out of the temperance movement and its members are called 'pioneers'. Every member has promised to abstain from alcohol. When young people make their confirmation they are encouraged to 'take the pledge' and not drink alcohol until they are at least eighteen. Many people continue to keep this pledge througout their entire lives.

Get Active 2

In groups create a PowerPoint® presentation on one of the following titles as an aid to teach the rest of the class about alcohol-related problems:

- ▶ How alcohol affects the individual
- ▶ How alcohol affects the family
- ▶ How alcohol affects the community
- ▶ Help that can be given to the individual and family
- ▶ Christian attitudes towards alcohol

2.3 Smoking and drugs

Smoking

Smoking was once socially acceptable and something that most people did. However, things are very different now. On Monday 30 April 2007 a smoking ban came into force in Northern Ireland. This made it illegal to smoke in workplaces, most public spaces and on public transport.

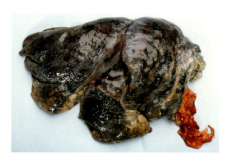

The diseased lung of a smoker

Why was there such a shift in people's opinions? Research! Research into smoking revealed the damage that it did to a person and how it shortened a person's life by ten years or more. It discovered that passive smokers, those who breathe in the smoke of others, were also in danger of developing smoking-related illnesses. It has now been established that smoking is the greatest single cause of illness and premature death in the UK.

So what does smoking do to you? The list is long and the following are just a few. To begin with your fingers become stained and your breath smells of nicotine. Your skin becomes wrinkled. Did you know that smokers have about ten times as many wrinkles as non-smokers? You can develop a sore throat and a hacking cough. You are more likely to develop lung cancer, stomach ulcers and have weak bones. Recent research has also shown that teenagers who smoke find it harder to concentrate in school as nicotine disrupts the development of nerve connections. Cigarette smoke contains over 4000 chemicals including 50 that are known to cause cancer. Listed below are some of these chemicals and what they are commonly used for.

- ▶ Acetone – found in nail polish remover
- ▶ Ammonia – found in household cleaning products
- ▶ Arsenic – a poison that can be lethal
- ▶ DDT – a chemical so harmful it has been banned from most uses (for example, insecticides)
- ▶ Formalin – a chemical used to preserve human remains
- ▶ Nitro benzene – a chemical often added to petrol
- ▶ Nicotine – the poisonous substance that makes smoking addictive.

Get Active 1

Working in groups, write a podcast that describes the effects smoking has on the human body and the chemicals that are found in cigarette smoke. Your podcast should be geared towards teenagers and interesting for them to listen to. It should be no longer than 30 seconds.

Legal drugs

All of us are drug users and drugs can be both helpful and harmful.
Thanks to medical research there are thousands of drugs that can be
taken when we are suffering from illness. These medicines can cure, slow
or prevent disease, helping us to lead healthier and happier lives.
Medicines are legal drugs. This means that doctors can prescribe them
for patients and some can be purchased in shops. However, it is not safe
for these medicines to be used in any way other than how they are
prescribed, or to buy them from people who are selling them illegally.
Other drugs that we can legally take are caffeine, nicotine and alcohol.

Many popular soft drinks contain caffeine

Illegal drugs

Illegal drugs include marijuana, ecstasy, cocaine, LSD, crystal meth and
heroin. How these drugs affect an individual depends on what the drug
is, how often it is used, how quickly it gets to the brain and how much is
taken. Also, whether other substances are taken at the same time,
differences in body size, shape, chemistry and the mood the person is in
when taking the drug. No two people are alike and how a drug affects
one person will not necessary be how it affects another.

The act of buying, selling, possessing and using drugs such marijuana is illegal

Why do people take illegal drugs?

There are many reasons why people choose to take illegal drugs. For
some young people it is the pleasure that they think they will experience.
For others it could be curiosity, to help them think better, be better
athletes or to gain attention from their parents. It may be peer pressure
and trying to fit in or trying to escape from how they feel and the
problems they are experiencing. However, rather than escaping from
their problems they are only creating new ones for both themselves and
their families.

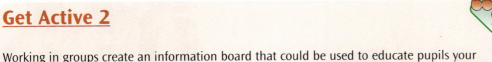

Get Active 2

Working in groups create an information board that could be used to educate pupils your
age about the dangers of taking drugs. Use the internet to gain more information. Ensure
that your board is interesting and uses pupil-friendly language.

2.4 Why work?

The answer to the question 'why do people work?' may seem obvious. Most people would say that they work to earn a living – to get enough money to provide a home, food, clothes, etc. for themselves and anyone else who depends on them (children, family). Why then do people who have enough money to provide everything they need still work? Some people who have won large sums of money on the National Lottery continue in the job they had before. There must be other reasons why people work.

Searching for a job in the classified section of a newspaper

Some other reasons may be:

a) To occupy our time

b) For self-respect and personal satisfaction

c) To pass on our knowledge and skills

d) For contact with other people

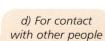

e) To fulfil our hopes and ambitions

f) To use our abilities and talents

Get Active 1

1 Individually choose one of the reasons from the speech bubbles opposite and write it into your notebook under the heading 'Why do people work?'.

2 Beside the text write two sentences explaining why you think this is a good reason for people working.

3 Find someone in your class who chose the same reason as you and discuss with them what you have written.

4 As a class discuss each of the reasons in turn. After the class discussion complete the following sentences in your notebooks:

   a Work is important in people's lives because...

   b I think it is important to work because...

For Christians, work is seen as an important aspect of a person's life and a way of serving God. The word '**vocation**' is often used to explain a person's choice of job. Many Christians believe that they have been given particular talents by God and that they have been called by God to do a certain job. This is also called their vocation. A vocation may mean that someone believes that God wants them to become a minister in a church or a missionary in another country. It could also mean using your talents in a different way – for example becoming a doctor or teacher.

Christians believe that whatever job they do, they should do this job to the best of their ability. There are a number of passages in the Bible that talk about work and working to the best of your ability as if you are working for God. These are given in the table below.

Get Active 2

1 Copy and complete the following table by reading the Bible passage and writing in what it says about work.

Passage	What does it say about work?
Jeremiah 1: 4–5	
Colossians 3: 23	
Genesis 2: 15	
Colossians 4: 1	
Ephesians 6: 5–7	

2 Working in groups using the magazines/newspapers you have been given, design and create a collage entitled 'Work'.

3 As a group write an explanation of your collage. Why have you chosen particular words/pictures for your collage? Why is work so important in our society? What are the religious views about work?

4 Explain your collage to the rest of the class. Display the collage and explanation.

Work in Islam and Buddhism

Christianity is not the only religion to place value on work. Many other religious faiths place an importance on the idea of working. Read the following information about Islam and Buddhism.

Muslims believe that it is a duty to work honestly and to the best of their ability. Skills that people have have been given to them by Allah, and it is important that they are used to benefit the community. The idea of community – UMMAH – is strong in Islam and everyone should work to benefit the community. As there are rules in Islam forbidding the use of alcohol there are also certain jobs that are forbidden. These include jobs relating to gambling, alcohol or illegal drugs and prostitution.

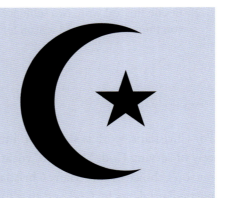

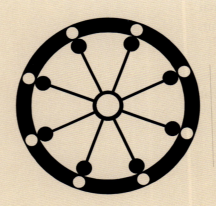

The Eightfold Path in Buddhism (see page 5) includes the guideline to have a 'right livelihood'. This means that Buddhists should choose the right job. They should choose a career that does not involve harming anyone else in any way. Buddhists believe that five kinds of job cause harm and should be avoided. They are:

► trade in deadly weapons

► trade in animals for slaughter

► trade in slavery

► trade in intoxicants

► trade in poisons.

Get Active 3

1 Work with a partner. Select one of the religions above and summarise their belief about work in two sentences. Place the information that you have in your workbook.

2 Now look at the other religion and summarise their belief about work in two sentences. Place the information that you have in your workbook.

3 Compare the information that you have and write one sentence to explain the similarities between the two religions' beliefs. Write one sentence to explain how the beliefs can be considered different.

4 Share your information with the rest of the class.

Free time – what should we do with it?

Religions also place importance on taking time to be with God and to spend with others in prayer.

In Christianity, Sunday is seen as the Sabbath day, the day of rest. Church services are held on a Sunday and this is a time for the Christian community to come together and worship God. For many Christians, working on a Sunday is breaking the fourth commandment.

In Islam, Muslims are given the duty to pray five times a day. The times are set according to the hours of daylight. Muslims may take time out from their work to pray to Allah. Muslims are encouraged to attend prayers at the mosque on a Friday at midday.

In Judaism, the Sabbath day runs from sunset on Friday evening until sunset on Saturday evening. Orthodox Jews will not work during this time. This includes cooking (which should be done in advance). Many Jewish families choose to live close to the synagogue so they can walk to services on the Sabbath.

A mosque - the Muslim place of worship

Get Active 4

Working in groups, discuss the information above, then copy and expand the three spider diagrams below (one for each religion). Think about the problems that members of the different religions may have following these rules in Northern Ireland today, the society that we live in and the demands that may be placed on people by their employers.

Think about any similarities between the religions and link up the diagrams by using arrows.

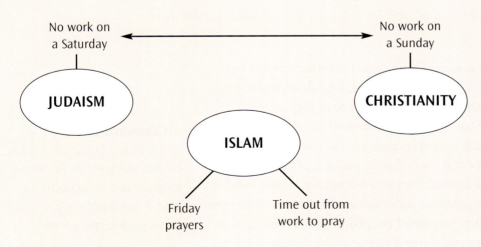

2.5 Our money/our future/ our choice

One reason given for people working is to earn enough money to provide for themselves or their families. We need a certain amount of money to buy food, pay bills, etc. but how should we spend the extra money that we have?

Enjoying a night out

People may want to enjoy a higher standard of living and have a more luxurious lifestyle. Also, some believe it is important to save a part of their income for their future or their family's future. Other people think it is important to give some of their income away to charities in order to help others.

Read the following statements and decide whether you agree or disagree with them.

a) 'Money makes the world go round.'

b) 'Whoever said money can't buy happiness simply didn't know where to go shopping.' (Bo Derek)

c) 'Time is more valuable than money.' (Jim Rohn)

d) 'Money is the root of all evil.'

Get Active 1

1   Write the statements above in your notebook under the headings – AGREE or DISAGREE.
2   Work individually. Imagine you had been given £100 to spend or save as you wished.
    a   How much money would you spend and what would you spend it on?
    b   Would you save any money? How much would you save?
    c   Would you give any of the money to charity? How much would you give?
    d   Write a short paragraph in your notebook to explain how you would use the money.

Within Christianity, money is seen as a gift from God which should be used in the right way. Just as God has given people the talents that they have to do their jobs, God has also provided the money they receive through the work they do. Many Christians believe that it is therefore important to give money back to God by giving to the church that they belong to. In the Old Testament it states that 10 per cent of a person's income was to be given back to God. This is called **tithing.** Some churches encourage their members to continue with this rule. In the New Testament no exact percentage or amount was stated but people were encouraged to set aside an amount that they could afford to give to the church.

> **2 CORINTHIANS 9: 7**
> *Each man should give what he has decided in his heart to give, not reluctantly or under compulsion, for God loves a cheerful giver.*

Get Active 2

Working in groups, discuss the information about tithing using the following question:
Do you think the 10 per cent guide for giving to the church is reasonable?

▶ Appoint a notetaker to write down the key points made in the discussion.

▶ Appoint a speaker to feed back the discussion to the rest of the class.

As well as giving to the church, many Christians also believe that it is important to give to charities where their money can be used to help others. There are vast numbers of charities that people could choose to support and it can sometimes be difficult to decide which ones deserve or need the money. People often choose to give to charities that they know most about which is why many charities now advertise or send out leaflets to people.

Get Active 3

1   Working in groups, look up the following websites to learn more about the work of these three Christian charities. Find out where the charities work, what they do to help people in need and how they use the money that people donate to them.

Tearfund – **http://youth.tearfund.org**

Christian Aid – **www.christianaid.org.uk**

Cafod – **http://kidzzone.cafod.org.uk**

2   Following your research discuss the charities in your group. You have to decide on one charity to support. Complete the following sentence on the poster paper provided:

We have chosen to support _____ because

_____

3   Share your sentence with the rest of the class.

Summary

▶ Christians believe that our bodies are the temple of the Holy Spirit and therefore should be looked after.

▶ Addiction is harmful to our minds as well as our bodies.

▶ People work for many different reasons not just to earn money.

▶ Christians believe that tithing their money is an important thing to do as everything they have is a gift from God.

Lifestyle choices: the big task

Now you have completed this chapter on 'Lifestyle choices', do the following task:

Look at the concept map below. It portrays global warming and what can be done to reduce it. A concept map combines key words, statements and illustrations to create a comprehensive overview of a topic.

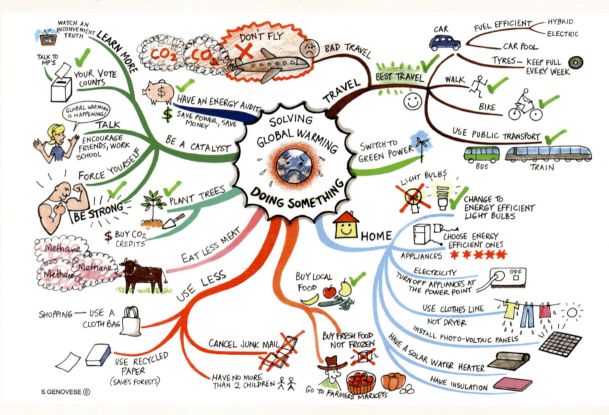

1 Create a concept map that illustrates the lifestyle choices discussed in this chapter.

In the centre of the page write 'Lifestyle choices' and draw a small illustration. Six branches should come from this entitled:

- Addiction
- Alcohol
- Smoking
- Drugs
- Work
- Money

2 Each branch should then be divided into separate branches with key words that explain and describe the titles above. A small illustration should accompany each key word. When your concept map is finished it should be a complete overview of the topic.

Chapter 3
Love in action

Learning intentions

I am learning:

▶ to understand that many people work to change unfair laws and situations because of the love they feel for people who are oppressed and marginalised

▶ about the work that five people did in order to change people's lives.

William Wilberforce

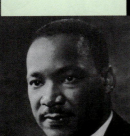

Martin Luther King

Elizabeth Fry

Oscar Romero

Lord Shaftesbury

Each of the people above is known as a **social reformer**. This means that they have been involved in trying to change unfair laws within their countries. Listed below is what each of them achieved. Try to link the person with the achievement.

1 Helped to reform prisons.

2 Gained equal rights for black people in America.

3 Helped to abolish slavery

4 Spoke out against their government and the treatment of the people.

5 Helped to stop child labour.

Within this chapter we shall take a closer look at each of these people and discover the work that they did.

3.1 Slavery – a thing of the past?

Slavery is the buying, selling and ownership of human beings for unpaid labour. In the past, slavery was a global trade. Many people from Africa and other continents were sold and forced to work without pay or freedom. In the past, religions allowed slavery to take place and there are passages in the Bible that suggest that slavery is acceptable. However in the eighteenth and nineteenth centuries the Christian **abolitionist** movement was important in ensuring that the slave trade and slavery was outlawed in the UK and eventually across the world.

African men, women and children being rounded up to be sold as slaves during the eighteenth century

Slaves working on a sugar plantation in the British West Indies during the nineteenth century

Get Active 1

Look at the images above of the slave trade in the eighteenth and nineteenth centuries. In your notebooks write a description of the conditions that the slaves had to endure from the information you can see in the images.

William Wilberforce (1759–1833)

William Wilberforce was a Member of Parliament in England. He became a Christian in 1784 and following a meeting with Thomas Clarkson (an abolitionist) he joined the Abolition of Slavery movement and became their voice in Parliament. However, those involved in the slave trade were very powerful and rich and it was difficult to get complete support to abolish the trade. In a speech to Parliament Wilberforce outlined the facts of how the trade worked and the terrible conditions that the slaves were forced to endure on the ships taking them across the Atlantic Ocean. At the end of the speech he said 'having heard all of this you may choose to look the other way but you can never say that you did not know'. It took a further 20 years of campaigning and a number of defeats before Parliament voted to abolish the slave trade. As a Christian, Wilberforce believed that slavery was wrong because all people are equal in the eyes of God.

Slavery in the modern world

Today slavery is outlawed across every country in the world but that does not mean that slavery is completely a thing of the past – in our world slavery still exists in a number of ways that are often described as forced bondage. Examples include:

'Conservative estimates indicate that at least 27 million people, in places as diverse as Nigeria, Indonesia and Brazil, live in conditions of forced bondage. Some sources believe the actual figures are 10 times as large.'
Richard Re, A Persisting Evil: The Global Problem of Slavery, Harvard International Review, *2002.*

▶ People being forced to work off a supposed debt – this may be their own debt or a family debt. This is called bonded labour. Many children can be forced into **bonded labour** because of a family debt.

▶ Passports can be confiscated from migrant workers to keep them in bondage.

▶ Human trafficking – women forced to work as prostitutes in different countries.

▶ Children forced to become child soldiers in wars.

Get Active 2

1 Look up the following websites to find out more about slavery today and campaigns to help people who have been forced into work.

www.antislavery.org/english/what_you_can_do/free_campaigns_resources.aspx

www.stopthetraffik.org/language.aspx

2 Working in groups, prepare a year assembly on the issue of slavery – past and present. You could include a drama/role play, poems, art and various religious passages.

3.2 Time for change

Other than the Queen only two women have appeared on a UK bank note. Florence Nightingale was on a ten pound note and Elizabeth Fry is on a five pound note. You may have heard of Florence Nightingale but how many of you know anything about Elizabeth Fry? In this topic we shall find out who she is and why she earned a place on the back of a five pound note.

Childhood

Elizabeth Gurney was born in Norwich on 21 May 1780. Both her parents came from banking families. Her father was a partner in the famous Gurney bank and her mother was a member of the Barclay banking family. She was raised as a Quaker and her mother insisted that her children spent two hours a day in silent worship. When she was twelve years old her mother died and as Elizabeth was one of the eldest girls she was expected to help bring up her younger brothers and sisters.

Social conscience

At eighteen Elizabeth met William Savery, an American Quaker, who was preaching in her town of Norwich. She was inspired by his words and decided to help those in need. Over the next few years she collected clothes for the poor, visited the sick and started a Sunday school in her summer house to teach the local children how to read.

At twenty Elizabeth married Joseph Fry, also a Quaker, and they had eleven children between 1801 and 1822. However, this didn't stop her work with those in need. When Stephen Grellet, a friend of the family, visited Newgate prison he was shocked by what he saw. Elizabeth decided to visit the women's section of the prison and was horrified at the conditions that the women were living in. Three hundred women and children were confined in a small area. They had to cook, wash and sleep in the same cell. They slept on the floor with no bedding or nightclothes. Some of the women had been found guilty of crimes, others were still waiting to be tried. Afterwards she wrote that:

> 'the swearing, gaming, fighting, singing and dancing were too bad to be described.'

Elizabeth Fry

Get Active 1

Look at the pictures below of two people who have appeared on bank notes. Do you know who they are? Why do you think they would be important enough to be on the back of a bank note?

Prison reform

Elizabeth began to visit the prison on a regular basis. She brought clothes and established a school for the children who were imprisoned with their parents. She also began a system of supervision that was administered by matrons and monitors and each woman was required to sew and to read the Bible. In 1817 she helped to found the 'Association for the Reformation of the Female Prisoners in Newgate'. This led to the creation of the 'British Ladies' Society for Promoting the Reformation of Female Prisoners'. This is widely believed to be the first nationwide women's organisation in Britain.

When Elizabeth's brother-in-law, Thomas Fowell Buxton, was elected to Parliament he began to promote her work among his fellow MPs. Elizabeth gave evidence to a House of Commons committee about the conditions in prison and was the first woman to present evidence in Parliament. The MPs were impressed by her work but disapproved of her view to abolish capital punishment. At that time people in England could be executed for over two hundred crimes, including cutting down trees, stealing a sheep or pickpocketing. Elizabeth and her brother, Joseph John Gurney, appealed to Lord Sidmouth, the Home Secretary, to reform the prison laws. However, he rejected their criticism of the prison system and in the House of Commons warned that Elizabeth and other reformers were dangerous people as they were trying to 'remove the dread of punishment in the criminal classes'.

When Sir Robert Peel became Home Secretary he listened to what Elizabeth had to say and introduced a series of reforms including the 1823 Gaols Act. Some of the reforms included prison wardens being paid, prison chaplains visiting regularly and female wardens being put in charge of female prisoners.

By 1820 Elizabeth had become well known all over Britain and at this time it was very unusual for a woman to be consulted by men for her professional knowledge. Elizabeth was not praised for her work but criticised in the press for neglecting her home and family.

Elizabeth Fry was a key figure in prison reform during the nineteenth century and it was her faith and the teachings of Jesus that inspired her to do all that she did.

Get Active 2

1 Explain how Elizabeth Fry's beliefs influenced her attempts to improve conditions for prisoners.

2 What problems affect prisons today and why might some people be motivated to work for prison reform?

3.3 Children's rights

In our society we often hear people talking about human rights and children's rights. In Northern Ireland every child has the right to education up to the age of sixteen and not to be exploited if they have a job. The campaign for children's rights started a long time ago with a man called Lord Shaftesbury (1801–1885). He lived at a time when even young children were working in factories, in coal mines and as chimney sweeps. As a Christian, Lord Shaftesbury believed that social reform was important and that children deserved a better start in life. He said:

> *'A man's religion … should enter every sphere of his life.'*

Lord Shaftesbury was a Member of Parliament and spent a lot of time campaigning so that very young children could be protected from having to work. In his lifetime, a number of laws were passed that meant that conditions gradually became better in the factories. He also supported the setting up of 'Ragged schools' where children were taught reading, writing and mathematics as well as learning about the Christian religion.

Lord Shaftesbury

Get Active 1

1   Look at the image to the right. Write a paragraph in your notebook about what the child in the picture is doing. Try to describe his clothes, the look on his face, and the work you think he may have had to do.

2   What do you think Lord Shaftesbury meant when he said 'A man's religion … should enter every sphere of his life'?

3   How did Lord Shaftesbury try to live out his Christian values through the work that he did?

The work of Lord Shaftesbury and others like him meant that slowly child labour was banned. All children in the UK are now given the opportunity to go to school before they begin their working life.

However, around the world today there are still many children working in poor conditions. Sometimes they earn very little money for the work that they do. They have to work long hours and are unable to attend school. According to the United Nations (UNICEF), there are an estimated 158 million children aged five to fourteen working worldwide. Families often rely on the money that the children earn for their own survival. The work may be in factories, on farms or even selling goods on the streets. Because they have to work, the children are often unable to attend school and therefore do not receive the education that they need to be able to do well in life.

Children as young as three breaking stones for road construction in Cambodia

Children working in a craft workshop in Kathmandu, Nepal

Get Active 2

1   Look at the images above of children working in the twenty-first century. What action do you think Lord Shaftesbury would take against this if he was alive today?

2   Use an internet search engine to find out more about child labour in the modern world. Select relevant information and images from your search and make notes. Use the images and information to write your own account about modern child labour. Write about what you think governments and other agencies should do to ensure that children are not exploited in this way.

3.4 Free at last

A significant historical event occurred on 20 January 2009 when Barack Obama was inaugurated as the forty-fourth president of the United States of America. Why was this significant? Because he was the first black president of the USA.

Only forty years earlier Martin Luther King was murdered because he was one of the leaders of the civil rights movement, working towards gaining equal rights for black people in the USA. Without the work of Martin Luther King and others like him, Barack Obama may never have been elected.

Who was Martin Luther King and why is he so important in the history of America?

President Barack Obama

Childhood

Martin Luther King was born on 15 January 1929 in Atlanta, Georgia. His father was a Baptist minister and Christianity heavily influenced Martin Luther King's thoughts and actions. Although he lived comfortably he realised at a young age that black and white people were treated differently. For example his two best friends went to a school at which only white children were permitted, and their parents no longer allowed Martin Luther King to play with them. His father was unable to buy him shoes unless he waited at the back of a shoe shop until it was empty of white customers – in some shops black people would only be served if they went to the back and waited there. The police never showed his family the respect that they gave to white families. This made Martin Luther King question his mother about it. She explained to him that black people had once been slaves and some white people considered black people inferior. Many white people didn't want to be in the company of black people and that was why a great number of schools, cafés, cinemas and even churches refused to let black people enter. However, Mrs King made sure that Martin Luther King knew that he was just as good as anyone else.

Martin Luther King

Get Active 1

Hot seat the following characters – a white police officer, Mr and Mrs King, a parent of one of the friends who was no longer allowed to play with Martin Luther King.

1   In groups of four think of one question to ask each of the characters and the answer that they might give.

2   Each person within the group should decide which character they would like to be.

3   Each group, in turn, should go to the front and the other groups ask each of the characters the questions they have thought of.

4   You should try to answer the question in the role of your character.

5   When a group has completed the question and answer session the rest of the groups should decide whether the answers given were correct.

Education

As a teenager Martin Luther King went to Morehouse College. This is a large secondary school with over 7000 pupils and was considered the best college for black pupils in America. The head teacher was a man called Dr Mays who was also a church minister. He talked to his pupils about how everyone was equal and how they should be fair to others. It was at this time that Martin Luther King began to realise that he wanted to help people and also teach them about Jesus. So at the age of seventeen he went to Crozer Theological Seminary and graduated in 1951 with a Bachelor of Divinity degree. While at Crozer he became interested in the teachings of Mahatma Gandhi. Gandhi had wanted India to be free from British rule but believed the only way to do this was through peaceful methods such as marches and strikes. Gandhi encouraged people to break unfair laws but always to be polite and peaceful. These ideas interested Martin Luther King and he felt that one day he could use them to help the black people of America. He went on to study at Boston University and graduated in 1955 with a PhD.

Get Active 2

Working in groups, type into an internet search engine 'Mahatma Gandhi for kids'. Use information from your search to write a short talk that briefly explains why Martin Luther King would be influenced by Mahatma Gandhi. Your talk should be no longer than one minute and everyone in the group must participate.

The beginnings of the civil rights movement

In 1954 Martin Luther King became the minister of a Baptist church in Montgomery, Alabama. The **segregation** of blacks and whites in Montgomery was very evident. For example, black people had to pay their bus fare at the front of the bus, then get off the bus and enter at the back and sit in the 'black section'. Even if the black section was full and the white section was empty the black people were only permitted in the area assigned to black people. However, if the bus was crowded and there were no seats in the white section a black person had to give their seat to the white passengers who did not have seats.

STRANMILLIS
UNIVERSITY COLLEGE
BELFAST

On 1 December 1955 Mrs Rosa Parks got onto a crowded bus. She found a seat at the front of the black passenger section but at the next stop when a white passenger got on the bus she was ordered to give her seat to him. She refused, the police were called and she was arrested.

Some of the black church ministers and leaders in Montgomery met to discuss the matter. They decided to ask all black people not to use buses on Monday 5 December. On Sunday 4 December the ministers asked their congregations to support their protest. The black people united and on Monday 5 December no black person travelled on the buses. This became known as the bus **boycott**. It meant that numerous black people had to get up early and walk many miles to work but they were prepared to make this sacrifice. The leaders of the bus boycott held a meeting and decided to call themselves the Montgomery Improvement Association (MIA). Martin Luther King was elected president. At this meeting it was decided that the bus boycott would continue until the unfair rules and segregation changed.

The bus boycott continued for over a year and during that time Martin Luther King and his family suffered a bomb attack on their home and received threatening phone calls and letters. Many of the black community found it difficult to stand by and watch as their leader was intimidated. After the bombing of his home an angry crowd gathered armed with broken bottles and guns. Some of them shouted insults at the police and trouble could have flared at any moment. King went out to talk to the crowd and told them that he wanted them to go home and put their weapons down. He said:

> 'We can't solve anything by violence. We must meet hate with love. Remember, if I am stopped, this movement will not stop. For God is with this movement.'

After that the crowd dispersed and a policeman was heard saying, 'if it hadn't been for that nigger preacher, we'd all be dead.'

At the end of 1956 the United States Supreme Court ruled that it was against the law of the country to maintain black and white segregation on the buses. Most people accepted the change but there were a few who were unhappy and continued to cause trouble for the black people. The buses were stoned. Black people were pulled off the buses and beaten up. Churches and homes were bombed. Regardless of this the bus boycott had been a success and black people now had the law on their side.

Even though the law stated that segregation on the buses was to stop there were still some parts of America in which this didn't happen. Subsequently in 1961 the 'freedom rides' started. Young people, both

Get Active 3

Imagine you are Rosa Parks. You have been asked to write an article for the local black newspaper to persuade people not to use the buses. Write down what you think you would say to encourage people to boycott the buses.

black and white, sat together on the buses that stated they should sit apart. They rode through the states together. However, many white people didn't like this and attacked the buses with stones and even fire bombs.

The **civil rights movement** continued to insist on equal rights for black people. In 1957 37,000 people, both black and white, took part in a freedom march in Washington. Martin Luther King spoke to the crowd and demanded that every black person should have the right to vote. Although it took eight years, in August 1965 the National Voting Rights Act was passed giving blacks the same rights as whites.

Martin Luther King (centre foreground) leads the Mississippi freedom marchers

In 1960 King decided to leave his job as a Baptist minister in Montgomery and devote more time to the civil rights movement. The headquarters of the movement was in Atlanta so he became joint minister at his father's church there. It was during this year that the 'sit-in' was used as a form of protest. Black and white people would 'sit-in' cafés and lunch counters together where they were supposed to sit apart. It was at this time that the song 'We Shall Overcome' became the song or anthem of the movement. However, many who participated suffered. For example, some were beaten up, burnt with cigarette butts and even arrested. King was in jail three times during 1960–1961. Despite this the 'sit-ins' were a success and hundreds of cafés and shops ceased segregation.

Martin Luther King delivering his famous 'I have a dream' speech

In August 1963 Martin Luther King led a march in Washington for 'jobs and freedom'. About 250,000 people took part in the march and, at the Lincoln Memorial, King addressed the vast crowd. It was here that he gave his famous 'I have a dream' speech. This march demonstrated to Americans that many people both black and white believed everyone was equal and should hold the same rights. However, there were those who continued to disagree with this, and less than a week after the Washington march a bomb went off in a church in Birmingham, Alabama, killing four black girls. Martin Luther King continued to receive death threats and when President Kennedy was murdered King told his wife that he feared he would also be murdered.

On Thursday 4 April 1968 Martin Luther King was in Memphis, Tennessee, to support the dustmen who were being unfairly treated by the new mayor. Just before he was to leave for the meeting he went out onto the balcony of his motel room. A shot rang out and King fell to the floor. The bullet had hit him in the neck. He was rushed to hospital but died one hour later. Martin Luther King had known his life was in danger and continued in spite of this knowledge, in the hope that he could help to achieve a better world for everyone to live in.

Get Active 4

1 Martin Luther King continued to work for the civil rights movement even though his life was in danger. Do you think he should have continued with his work? Explain your answer.

2 Should religious people become involved in political issues and cause mass disruption to a country in order to change unfair laws? Explain your answer.

3 Explain how the work of Martin Luther King and others like him laid the path for the election of a black president in the USA.

3.5 Set free the oppressed

A dictionary definition of **oppression** is 'to control by cruelty or force'. Throughout history there have been a number of governments or armies who have been accused of oppressing the people living in their countries. One man who lived under an oppressive government was Archbishop Oscar Romero. He lived in El Salvador and was assassinated in 1980 because he spoke out against the government for killing many of the poor farmers living in the country.

El Salvador

El Salvador is a small country in Central America where the majority of people are poor farmers called **campesinos**. Between 1970–80 there was a big gap between the rich who ruled the country and poor farmers. The campesinos were often treated very badly by the ruling government and army with many people losing their lives because they spoke out against the government. The USA gave military aid to the government at this time. By the beginning of the 1980s there was a civil war in the country which lasted until 1992.

Archbishop Oscar Romero

Oscar Romero was made Archbishop of San Salvador, the capital of El Salvador, in 1977. The campesinos did not expect Romero to stand up for them but shortly after he became Archbishop, his friend, another priest, was killed by the army. This changed Romero's thinking and he began to speak up for the poor in the country. He organised demonstrations and used his weekly sermons to speak out against the government and the actions of the army. This did not stop the oppression. In 1980, while Romero was celebrating Mass in a hospital chapel he was assassinated by a sniper's bullet.

As Archbishop, Romero believed that he was following the teaching of Jesus in speaking up for the oppressed in his country. He used his position in the Christian Church, not only in El Salvador, but across the world to speak up for people who could not speak up for themselves. Here are some of the things he said:

'One must not love oneself so much, as to avoid getting involved in the risks of life that history demands of us, and those that fend off danger will lose their lives.'

'If some day they take away the radio station from us … if they don't let us speak, if they kill all the priests and the bishop too, and you are left a people without priests, each one of you must become God's microphone, each one of you must become a prophet.'

'The world of the poor teaches us that liberation will arrive only when the poor are not simply on the receiving end of hand-outs from governments or from the churches, but when they themselves are the masters and protagonists of their own struggle for liberation.'

'I do not believe in death without resurrection. If they kill me, I will be resurrected in the Salvadorean people.'

Get Active 1

Group discussion:

1   Read the quotations from Romero's sermons while he was Archbishop and discuss what they mean. Choose one of the quotations and put it into your own words.

2   Discuss how you think Romero was able to put the teaching of Jesus and his own teaching into action.

The life of Oscar Romero has not been forgotten by the people that he represented. He is still greatly respected by the people of El Salvador as a **martyr** who gave his life for the people he represented. Over the last few decades the people of El Salvador have used the symbol of the cross to promote their fight for justice and freedom.

Get Active 2

Using images from newspapers or magazines create your own collage of the symbol of the cross and entitle it 'Justice and freedom'.

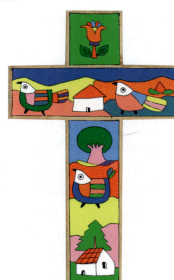

Salvadorean painted crucifix

Summary

▶ Through persistence William Wilberforce abolished slavery after 20 years of campaigning. However, throughout the world today illegal slavery still continues in different forms.

▶ Elizabeth Fry was horrified at the conditions women were kept in when she visited a women's prison. She faced much opposition when she brought her proposed prison reforms to Parliament. However, she was not deterred and continued to campaign until the laws were changed.

▶ Through the work of Lord Shaftesbury and others like him children in the UK and Ireland can enjoy free education without the worry of having to work to support their families.

▶ Martin Luther King was one of the key figures who led the civil rights movement in America.

▶ Oscar Romero believed that he had to be the voice of his people who were being oppressed. Although loved by his people, the Salvadorean government didn't like what he had to say and he was assassinated.

Love in action: the big task

Complete a project on one of the social reformers discussed in this chapter. Your project should contain the following:

▶ personal background – childhood, family, education, etc.

▶ the work they were involved in, how they sought to change the law and the outcome of their work

▶ their faith

▶ how belief in Jesus' teachings about love influenced the work of these reformers.

1 Before you begin the project agree a set of success criteria with the class that will guarantee that this is a successful piece of work.

2 Ensure that you do some research and don't just use the information found in the textbook.

3 When the project is completed choose a partner and read their project. Decide whether all the success criteria were met. If any criteria are missing discuss this with your partner. If all the criteria are met does this make the project a successful piece of work? Explain your opinions to your partner.

Chapter 4
Does God exist?

Learning intentions

I am learning:

▶ to describe who we each think God is

▶ to explore arguments for and against the existence of God

▶ to understand the issues of natural and moral evil

▶ to discuss how people experience God in different ways.

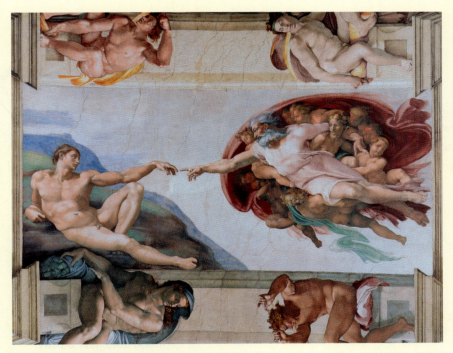

The Creation of Adam by Michelangelo

Discuss

1   Look at the image above. Do you agree with the image of God that the artist has created?

2   What is the traditional image that people often have of God? Do you think this is right?

4.1 Who is God?

Get Active 1

Answer the questions in the spider diagram below.

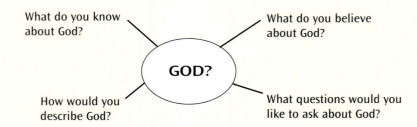

What do you know about God?

What do you believe about God?

GOD?

How would you describe God?

What questions would you like to ask about God?

Who is God?

Christians describe God as an all-powerful being who has no beginning or end. God exists outside of time and space and is responsible for the creation of our world, galaxy and universe. Some words that can be used to describe God are:

▶ **Omnipotent**: unlimited power

▶ **Omnipresent**: present everywhere

▶ **Omniscient**: all-knowing.

If these are words that Christians use to describe God then what does God look like?

Many Christians believe that God is a 'spirit' without physical form which enables God to be all-powerful, all-knowing and everywhere. However, what do they mean when they refer to God as a 'spirit'?

They don't mean some sort of ghostly form, as ghosts may have some shape. They believe that God is an invisible force whose power can be seen within the world. Can you think of other forces of power that can be seen and felt but are invisible to the human eye?

Get Active 2

Draw a picture of what you think God looks like and explain why you have drawn God like this.

Think …

Does God have a body?

If God does have a body how would this limit God's power and ability?

If God doesn't have a body what does God look like?

The power of the wind can be seen and felt but it is an invisible force. For example, your teacher is unable to go into the playground on a windy day, collect some wind in a jar and bring it into your class for you to see. Yet you know it exists because it can be felt blowing through your hair and heard rustling through the trees.

Electricity is another example of an invisible force that we use every day.

Just like wind and electricity Christians believe that God's power can be seen through creation and felt in their lives. Yet God's power is quite different. It is a loving, thoughtful, caring and creative force. The wind doesn't

The wind is a powerful force of nature that we can feel but cannot see directly

whip around a pillar of stone and create a beautiful sculpture, neither does lightning strike a tree to create a wonderful carving. Wind and electricity don't have caring, thoughtful minds that are concerned about the people they touch. Christians believe God does care.

The existence of wind and electricity are not in dispute because they are known, proven forces within our world which everyone has experienced and which scientists can explain, measure and predict. The same cannot be said about God. There are many different attitudes towards God and the following are three of the most common:

Theist: someone who believes that there is a God
Atheist: someone who believes that there is no God
Agnostic: someone who doesn't know if there is a God or not.

A lightning strike in a city. There are some 16 million lightning storms in the world every year

4.2 Proof of God

Many people state that they don't believe in God because they feel there is insufficient or no proof that he exists. This is not a new debate and Christians throughout the ages have put forward arguments that they believe proves the existence of God. Three of these are outlined below.

Arguments for the existence of God

The cosmological argument

Thomas Aquinas, a Christian monk, lived 800 years ago and put forward his argument which became known as 'the cosmological argument' or 'the first cause argument'. He stated that by looking at the world and the universe we see things moving. Things are unable to move by themselves, something has to put them into motion. However, we cannot look back to infinity as there would be no starting movement and therefore no second movement. Consequently, Thomas Aquinas stated that it all had to start somewhere, with something, and that starting point was God.

The design argument

William Paley, 1743–1805 stated that the design of the world proves that God exists. There is order to the universe and this couldn't just have happened – someone must have created it. He explains it like this: If you were out for a walk and tripped over a rock, you wouldn't question its existence but merely accept that it was there. However, if you were out walking and found an old fashioned watch with wheels, cogs and springs working together to tell the time, you wouldn't just accept its existence. Rather the complexity of the watch would force you to believe that there was a designing mind behind it. He compares this with the eye. The eye is a complex structure which could not have come about by chance. It had to be designed in order for it to work as it does.

Religious experience

Some Christians state that their proof of God is in the personal experiences they have of him. This is something that is very difficult to prove or disprove. This can be likened to our emotions. Love is something that we feel towards someone but how do we prove to others that we are experiencing it? Some Christians would say that God can be seen in nature, for example, the sheer beauty of a sunset or the majesty of the mountains.

Get Active 1

Read questions 1 and 2, which both contain two parts. For each question answer the part that relates to your beliefs. Then answer question 3.

1 Which of the above arguments do you agree with and why? Or you may not agree with any of them. Explain why.

2 How would you try to prove that God exists? Or you may not believe that God exists. Explain why.

3 Can you see any faults with the above arguments? What are they?

Do these arguments prove the existence of God?

The cosmological argument

This argument states that something cannot come out of nothing, and that there had to be a beginning to all movement. However, it seems to contradict itself as it believes and accepts that God came from nothing and always existed! Other people who disagree with this argument state that they accept that there had to be a starting point but that starting point doesn't have to be God. Still others argue that our experiences are limited to what happens within our world, and things outside of our world and universe could happen completely differently.

Think ...
Can you think of any other arguments against this one?

The design argument

This argument states that the order of our world points to a designer. However, some people would argue that as humans we have imposed an order on things to make them manageable. In places were there is chaos we have created an illusion of order to make us feel better. Others would state that the design of the world seems to have flaws such as earthquakes, volcanoes, hurricanes, etc. Why would a good God design a world like that?

Think ...
Can you think of any other arguments against this one?

Hurricane damage on an island in the Carribean

Discuss

Organise a class debate entitled 'Proof of God'.

Religious experience

This argument states that people have had a personal experience of God that proves to them that God exists. However, people who disregard this argument state that there is no proof that those who have had these experiences are actually telling the truth. They also state that if God gives religious experiences to some people why not to everyone?

Think ...
Can you think of any other arguments against this one?

4.3 The problem of evil

Some people state that if God is an all-powerful, all-loving God he would not allow evil things to happen. Therefore they conclude that God must not exist because there is evil in our world that causes pain and suffering to the people living in it. Many people think that evil can be divided into two groups – **natural evil** and **moral evil**. Natural evils are things that happen outside the control of humans, for example, hurricanes, tsunamis, volcanoes. Moral evils are human-made evils.

In volcanic eruptions rivers of molten rock or huge clouds of ash are released

Get Active 1

In groups complete the following task:

1 Write down different things that cause people to suffer.
2 Divide the list into natural evils, moral evils or a combination of both.
3 Which type of evil occurs the most? Is this a true reflection of life? Explain your answer.

Think …
What sort of world would you prefer to live in? A perfect world where everyone is created to always do what God wants or the world we live in where people have a free will and can do as they please even if it causes suffering. Why?

Moral evil

Christians believe that when God created humans he did not want to make robots merely programmed to do what he wanted. God wanted the people he had made to choose to do his will because they loved him. He therefore provided them with the gift of **free will** – the ability to choose how to act – rightly or wrongly. With the gift of free will came a great responsibility to act in a loving fashion towards other people. However, as can regularly be seen in the world, humans choose to act selfishly and often make decisions that enable them to be happy, regardless of the suffering caused to others. God does not intervene in the decisions that people make even if it causes great suffering to others because any intervention would take away their free will.

Moral evil is the suffering that results from the bad choices made by people misusing their free will.

Natural evil

The power of Mother Nature continues to astound us. The destruction caused by wind, water, fire and earth is often frightening. Illnesses, with the pain and suffering they bring, often terrify us and because of this many cannot accept that a loving God exists.

Most of the natural evils that occur are not evil in themselves. They become evil when humans suffer as a result of them. In order for our world to exist in its present form, many of these natural evils have to happen. Earthquakes are caused when the tectonic plates move and rub together. Volcanic eruptions are caused when the pressure of molten rock, known as lava, and gas becomes too much, and they are released through vents in the earth's crust, known as volcanoes. Many people choose to live near volcanoes because of the fertile land even though they know the volcano could erupt at some time in the future. Many of the floods, droughts and hurricanes caused by natural weather patterns happen in parts of the world that also have great conditions for growing crops.

Others believe that suffering exists in the world because it is only through these tough times that we become stronger. In other words, if we never had to face pain then qualities such as perseverance, courage and empathy would never develop. People would remain immature individuals, laughing their way through life as if nothing could go wrong and there would be no serious consequences to their actions. By experiencing the challenges of this world we become more spiritually mature and more like the person God ultimately wants us to be.

Flooding can destroy homes and lead to health problems

Mudslides can be very sudden and destructive

A forest fire can spread very quickly and be hard to contain

Get Active 2

1 What sort of friend would you prefer to have – a robot friend that does everything you ask and goes wherever you want or a friend with a free will? Explain your answer.

2 Explain why God chose to give humans free will.

3 What have been the consequences of giving humans free will? Explain your answer.

4 Explain the difference between natural evil and moral evil.

5 Christians believe that the origins of evil are explained in Genesis 3: 1–24. Read the passage and describe how evil first came into the world.

6 The passage in Genesis raises some interesting questions. Write down any questions you would like to ask and discuss them with the class.

4.4 Experiencing God

Get Active 1

Look at the images above and think about the ways that Christians believe that they can experience God in their lives. Copy and complete the spider diagram to the right, adding as many ways of experiencing God as possible.

Prayer

Experiencing God

There are many ways in which people believe they have experienced God. This could include God answering their prayers in some way, speaking through other people, through events that have happened in their lives or through worship and prayer. The Bible is full of examples of God talking directly to people and intervening in their lives in some way.

The prophet Elijah

Elijah was a messenger from God in the Old Testament. He was in trouble because Queen Jezebel had ordered his death as he had defeated the god that she worshipped. He was so scared he wanted to die. Elijah fled to the mountains and believed that he was the only true follower of God left in all of Israel. He felt he had been deserted. God told him that he would speak to him. God sent three powerful forces of nature – a great wind, an earthquake and fire; however he did not speak through these. Finally God spoke in a whisper and told Elijah he was not on his own. He was given instruction as to what to do next.

Get Active 2

1 Read the full story of Elijah's experience in 1 Kings 19: 1–14.

2 Working in pairs, think of five questions that you have about this passage.

3 Join another pair – look at each other's questions and try to answer them together.

Saul's experience of God

Another example of someone experiencing God in a dramatic way comes from the New Testament. Shortly after the death and resurrection of Jesus his followers began to preach about what had happened. They were persecuted by the Jewish leaders in Jerusalem. One of the main persecutors was a Pharisee called Saul. He wanted all followers of Jesus to be arrested and travelled from Jerusalem to the town of Damascus to capture anyone preaching about Jesus. However, on the road to Damascus he had an unexpected experience of God.

Saul became one of the most important leaders of the early Christian Church. He changed his name to Paul and travelled across the Roman Empire to preach about Jesus. He also wrote a number of letters to people in the churches he had set up and these are included in the New Testament.

Get Active 3

1 Read the story of Saul's experience of God in Acts 9: 1–19.

2 Imagine you are Ananias and you have been asked to go to Saul – write an account about what happened and what you think will be the consequences of Saul's conversion.

4.5 Does God speak to people today?

People often argue that God does not speak today the way he spoke to people like Elijah and Paul in the Bible. They therefore find it hard to believe that God is still working in the world. However, Christians believe that God still speaks today and that it is important for people to listen to God in their everyday lives. They believe that God guides people in their lives and that he helps them through times of trouble, sickness and even through the death of those they love.

Mabel Colson-Brown believes that God spoke to her and told her to go to Brazil as a missionary. This is what she says about the experience:

> *'Trust me to go to a missionary conference on Africa. The speaker, in full flow about the need in Africa, made a quick mention of Brazil, "Oh they need teachers in Brazil". Wham! God spoke to me through those unexpected words. I don't think I heard anything else. I was to go to Brazil. I felt such peace about it. Others in the church, after much prayer, confirmed that it was God's will and two years later off I went (Paul didn't have as many committees and interviews to deal with!). Knowing it was God who told me to go to Brazil also became my strength to overcome the difficulties when there.'*

During her time in Brazil Mabel worked on an indigenous Indian reservation as a teacher in a Bible college. She had to learn Portuguese and adapt to the heat and unfamiliar ways of a different culture. Throughout she believes that she experienced God in a number of different ways. Here is one example:

> *'I saw Xuxa walking to her house. "Give her the money you took out of the bank today." I knew it was God speaking. So, I called her and, all embarrassed, said "God wants you to have this". She looked confused, I went red and left. A few hours later she told me she needed surgery but couldn't pay for it. The money God told me to give her was the exact amount for the first payment. If God could give her that, surely he would pay for the rest. Well he did! Obey the voice you hear. "My sheep know my voice" (John 10: 4).*

Get Active 1

Working in groups, discuss Mabel's experiences of God using the following questions. Appoint a scribe to write down the main points made in the discussion and someone to feed back to the rest of the class.

1 In what different ways has Mabel's experience of God changed her life?

2 How has Mabel's faith in God helped her to trust her actions?

3 How is Mabel's experience of God similar to Elijah and Paul's experiences of God?

Declan O'Loughlin is a priest working in the Archdiocese of Armagh. He spent many years teaching Religious Education in Dublin and later in Dundalk. He is the Diocesan Adviser for Religious Education for the Catholic post primary schools of the Archdiocese and resides in the small parish of Dromintee in South Armagh.

Declan has worked with young people throughout his **ministry** and leads a weekly Taizé prayer meeting in his home every Wednesday evening. Declan describes this weekly gathering as his own spiritual bread and butter and finds praying together with others a rich experience and one of life's great blessings. He has recorded some **meditations** based on the gospel for use by school groups and people living at home or in hospital. Currently he is working on a recording of the 'Jesus prayer' as a way of helping people meet the living God in the rush of everyday life. This is what he says about experiencing God in his life:

Father Declan O'Loughlin

'All the great teachers about God encourage us to spend time each day talking to God. One realises that doing is better than speaking about it. For me God is revealed in a very unique way in the person of Jesus of Nazareth. When I pray I find myself remembering a story about Jesus and placing myself in the picture. I then find the words spoken seem always to be spoken to me. He challenges me to give up my own wealth and personal agenda and spend my time reaching out to be there for others as he did so much in his life here on earth. Other days I think of God as a family of three persons who have a special place for me in their circle of friendship. When you travel on the tube in London there is an announcement to "mind the gap" in case you fall down onto the line. I believe these three wonderful people in God ask me to fill a gap they have created from all eternity for me to fill … mind-blowing really yet ever so true. My life's purpose is one day to share the very circle of God's own life of love. So God is for me a real daily experience of being in the presence of the people who love me most of all in the universe. The fact that my family and friends love me is a reminder to me that what they do by their love for me is a reflection of who and what God really is. Paul says we see the life in God like looking in a dark mirror now but that one day we will see God in all of the beauty and love that God is. I say … mind the gap!'

Get Active 2

1   Read through the information about Mabel and Declan's personal experiences of God. Discuss with your partner the different ways in which God has spoken to them in their lives.

2   Make a list of five questions about ways in which people experience God in their lives using the information on these pages to help.

3   Discuss the questions as a class and decide on the five most important questions.

4   Invite a local minister or priest to answer the questions to find out more about personal experiences of God.

4.6 Mystical experiences

Across the world, in various religions, people see **mystical** experiences as the ultimate experience of God – seeking a direct experience of God. This can be seen throughout religions in a number of different ways, for example, Sufism in Islam and Kabbalah in Judaism.

Sufism

Sufism is a branch of Islam and is seen as an inner mystical dimension. It was described by Amad Ibn Ajiba, a Moroccan Sufi and writer, as 'a science through which one can know how to travel in the presence of the Divine'. One of the most common images of a Sufi is the 'whirling dervish' from Turkey. The whirling is seen as a method to reach religious ecstasy. However, this is only one aspect. Sufism has strict rules that inform the actions that followers can take in their lives.

Dervish
by the poet Rumi

Water that's poured inside will sink the boat while water underneath keeps it afloat.

Driving wealth from his heart to keep it pure King Solomon preferred the title poor.

That sealed jar in the stormy sea out there floats on the waves because it's full of air.

When you've the air of dervishhood inside you'll float above the world and there abide.

Get Active 1

Use an internet search engine to find out more about Sufism and the 'whirling dervish'. Note down useful information for use in Get Active 2.

Kabbalah

As Sufism is a branch of Islam, so Kabbalah is a branch of Judaism. It is seen as a mystical aspect of Judaism that seeks to define the nature of the universe and human beings. Kabbalahism has hit the headlines recently as a number of celebrities including Madonna, Demi Moore and Britney Spears have all studied aspects of Kabbalah.

Like all religious traditions, Kabbalah looks to help people discover meaning in their life. There are many different levels to Kabbalah and many symbols that are used to represent the mystic nature of human beings and God. These symbols include the 'Tree of Life' and the 'Thirteen Petalled Rose'.

Rabbi Steinsaltz has written a book called *The Thirteen Petalled Rose* and in it he explores the relationship that humans have with God through the mystic ideas of Kabbalah:

Madonna

Kabbalah bracelet

> 'This little book is a book for the soul. It begins, quite deliberately (and perhaps to the dismay of some readers), with a view of another reality. It does not proceed from this world. Instead, it seeks to go from the genuine centre of all being to the world and to human life. If a person permits his soul to listen, the soul will soon learn that all it needs to do is remember. Because in some dim and enigmatic way, it already knows all this.'
>
> (Rabbi Steinsaltz, *The Thirteen Petalled Rose* (1992)

Within Kabbalah, study of the book of *Zohar*, meditation and further teaching is important.

Get Active 2

Use an internet search engine to find out more about Kabbalah. Note down useful information. Use the information that you have on Sufism and Kabbalah to write a newspaper article about the two religions. Your article should be no more than 300 words and should include:

▶ a headline – to make people want to read your piece

▶ images relating to the information that you have

▶ mystical experiences within Sufism and Kabbalah which bring people closer to God

▶ an appropriate layout.

Summary

▶ It is difficult to describe God but Christians see him as a spirit – all-knowing, all-powerful and everywhere.

▶ There are a number of arguments for and against the existence of God that have been developed by people over many centuries.

▶ People who do believe in God experience him in a number of ways in their lives.

▶ Different religious groups believe that they can experience God and come closer to him through prayer, meditation, dancing and study.

Does God exist?: the big task

Now you have completed this chapter on 'Does God exist?' do the following task:

Write an argumentative piece under the heading 'Does God exist?' Use the information from the chapter to help you structure and write your essay. Your essay should include:

▶ An introduction outlining the purpose of your writing.

▶ Paragraphs outlining a number of arguments for and against the existence of God. You may wish to give examples from this chapter of people's personal experience of God to back up arguments.

▶ A conclusion – answer the question from your own perspective and give reasons for your point of view.

Chapter 5
Sectarianism and reconciliation

Learning intentions

I am learning:

▶ to explore the definition of sectarianism

▶ to discuss the consequences of sectarianism in Northern Ireland and across the world

▶ about examples of reconciliation that bring differing groups together in order to bring an end to sectarian conflict

▶ to explore the work of the Corrymeela community and their hopes for the future of Northern Ireland.

1

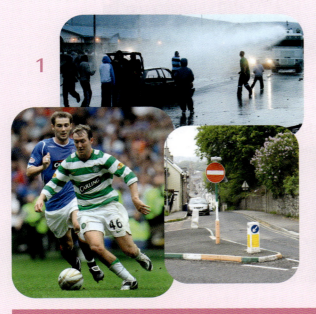

2

Discuss

Working as a group discuss the images above. Which group of images do you most associate with living in Northern Ireland? Why?

5.1 Sectarianism – a thing of the past?

Sectarianism is an issue that is often talked about in Northern Ireland. After over thirty years of unrest, the peace process has at last brought some stability and prosperity to Northern Ireland. However, do we still live in a society divided by sectarianism because of religious differences?

Wikipedia's definition of sectarianism is as follows:

'Sectarianism is bigotry, discrimination or hatred arising from attaching importance to perceived differences between subdivisions within a group, such as between different denominations of a religion or the factions of a political movement.'

Republican mural, Falls Road, West Belfast

Loyalist mural, Sandy Row, Belfast

Sectarianism is seen as intolerance of a differing point of view within religions. In Northern Ireland this has been demonstrated within Christianity – between the Roman Catholic and Protestant denominations.

Get Active 1

1   Working in groups, look at the pictures and information above. Discuss the following question in your group:

    What evidence do we have that sectarianism exists in Northern Ireland?

2   Use a large sheet of poster paper to draw, write or symbolise the actions, thoughts or words that can be used to explain how sectarianism happens.

3   As a class discuss your posters. Make a smaller poster in your notebook using examples from the different posters in the class, underneath the heading 'What evidence do we have that sectarianism exists in Northern Ireland?'

Catholics and Protestants – what's the difference?

Protestants and Catholics belong to the same Christian faith and have many of the same beliefs.

They all believe that:

▶ Jesus is the Son of God

▶ Jesus was born of a virgin

▶ Jesus lived his life preaching, healing and teaching others

▶ Jesus was crucified in order to save people from their sins; and that he rose again from the dead.

Both Roman Catholics and Protestants have the same Christian values of love, forgiveness, care for others, justice and peace.

The differences between the Churches are often misunderstood and these can be seen as divisions. The Protestant and Roman Catholic Churches have some differences in how they worship and have differing interpretations as to how Churches should be run:

Pope Benedict XVI

▶ Roman Catholics believe that his Holiness the Pope is the leader of the Church and that he speaks on behalf of God. Protestants do not believe the Pope speaks on God's behalf and do not accept him as their leader.

▶ Roman Catholics believe that when they are given the bread at communion it changes – in a spiritual way – into the body of Jesus. Protestants view the bread as symbolic of the body of Jesus and do not accept that it changes.

Are these differences the cause of sectarianism? The issue of sectarianism goes much deeper than these differences. There is a long history of mistrust that stems back to the **Reformation** in the sixteenth century. This is when some Christians split from the Roman Catholic Church and a number of new denominations were formed. At different times in history one group felt mistreated by the other and so mistrust and division grew across generations.

Get Active 2

1   Use the following website to find out more about sectarianism in Northern Ireland. Use your notebook to write down important facts that you discover through your research. There are a number of different activities that you can complete from the following website: **www.bbc.co.uk/northernireland/ learning/eyewitness/sectarian/ index.shtml**

2   Following your research write a short account (about 200 words) of the issues that people in Northern Ireland face because of sectarianism. At the end answer the following question 'Is sectarianism in Northern Ireland about religion?'

5.2 The consequences of sectarianism

In Northern Ireland we are very aware of the consequences of sectarian attitudes. It has caused a number of problems for people from different areas – in cities, towns and in the country. However, sectarianism is not just an issue for Northern Ireland. There are countries across the world where problems have arisen because of religious differences and intolerance leading to sectarian attitudes.

Islam, like Christianity, has two major denominations – Sunni and Shia. This division dates back to the death of the founder of Islam, Muhammad (PBUH) and the arguments about who would succeed him as the leader of the Muslim faith. Over the centuries further differences have emerged in terms of leadership and some cultural differences.

For over 1000 years Sunni and Shiite Muslims have been divided and Iraq has often been the centre of this division. There are many more Shiite than Sunni Muslims living in Iraq, however, under Saddam Hussein, Sunni Muslims dominated the political and economic life of the country persecuting the Shiite majority.

However, this dominance ended with the invasion of Iraq by the US-led coalition as Shiite leaders took greater power as the majority within the country. This has raised the sectarian tension between the two denominations and attacks on Shiite targets have become common.

Sunni extremists have begun to attack the Shiite majority, especially their most important shrines at Karbala, Najaf and Samara. They have killed many Shiite politicians, clerics, police and soldiers, raising the tension even higher.

Get Active 1

1 Read the article on the opposite page and answer the following questions in your notebook:

   a What is the main cause of sectarianism within Iraq?

   b Why do you think Sunni and Shiite Muslims are involved in attacks against each other?

   c What are the consequences of the attacks?

   d Is the sectarianism within Iraq solely based on the religious differences between the two groups?

2 Discuss your answers with the rest of the class.

Bombs kill at least 28 near Baghdad mosque

Bombs near five Shiite mosques killed at least 28 people across Baghdad on Friday, police said …

The blasts, which wounded at least 130 people, appeared to target Shiite Muslims taking part in Friday prayers and were a reminder of the capabilities of militants despite the sharp drop in violence over the last 18 months in Iraq.

In the worst attack, a car bomb killed at least 23 people praying in the street near the crowded al-Shurufi mosque in northern Baghdad's Shaab district …

After the blast, blood soaked the ground and stained prayer mats outside the mosque. The site was littered with abandoned slippers. The charred skeleton of a car sat nearby.

Shiite religious gatherings have been targets of Sunni Islamist al Qaeda, which regards Shiites as heretics …

On the other side of the city, two blasts went off around the same time near a mosque in southeastern Baghdad's Diyala bridge area, killing four people.

Another car bomb in Zaafaraniya, southeast Baghdad, killed one person. Two more bombs close to mosques in Kamaliya and Alam districts wounded nine people.

Iraqis carry dead bodies on a pushcart outside a Shiite mosque in Baghdad following a suicide bombing

'Those who carried out these acts targeting the faithful are the enemies of Iraq, without principles or values,' said Major-General Abboud Qanbar, head of Iraqi forces in Baghdad …

US officials say al Qaeda and other Sunni insurgent groups, most active in ethnically mixed areas north of Baghdad, are trying to reignite the sectarian conflict that brought Iraq to the brink of all-out civil war in 2006 and 2007.

31 July 2009 uk.reuters.com

Although sectarianism is seen as based on religious differences there are often a number of other factors involved, such as political viewpoints and community differences – religious differences can often be used as an excuse for disputes which go much deeper.

Get Active 2

Organise and conduct a class debate on the statement:

'This House agrees that religion is the sole cause of sectarianism in the world today.'

You may wish to spend some time researching other sectarian conflicts across the world. Ensure that everyone in the class has a role to play within the debate. Discuss with your teacher how to set up the debate and the roles that everyone should take.

5.3 Reconciliation

Reconciliation is the opposite of sectarianism. It attempts to bring the opposing sides together in order to talk about the pain that has been caused, to seek forgiveness from each other and to find ways to move forwards collectively.

Apartheid and the Truth and Reconciliation Commission

Over the last few years many countries which have been divided along sectarian lines have decided to embrace reconciliation techniques in order to help the communities come to terms with what has happened to them and their families. The most famous of these is the South African 'Truth and Reconciliation Commission' (TRC) set up in 1995 after the abolition of **apartheid**.

The commission, which was led by Archbishop Desmond Tutu, invited people from both sides to come forward and be heard. Those who felt that they had been victims of the violence during apartheid and those who had committed the acts of violence and genuinely felt remorse for what they had done were invited to tell their stories. Many people who had committed acts of violence came forward to be heard and sought **amnesty** from prosecution. Over 7000 people sought amnesty, over 5300 were refused and approximately 800 were granted amnesty. Those who sought amnesty came face to face with the relatives of those they had killed. These relatives listened as they sought forgiveness and then they had to decide whether they could forgive them or not. This was not an easy process, but at a basic level reconciliation begins with individuals finding the strength to forgive and move on.

The South African Truth and Reconciliation Commission

Get Active 1

Imagine you have been asked by the Truth and Reconciliation Commission to come to a hearing where you will have to listen to someone ask for your forgiveness for the death of your brother. Write two accounts in your diary:

▶ The first is the night before the hearing. Explain your feelings and emotions towards the accused. Describe how you feel about going to the hearing and whether it is something that you feel will help in the healing process.

▶ The second is the night after the hearing. How did you feel listening to the accused? Did you decide to forgive him? Explain your decision.

As with any process there were those who thought that it was successful in starting a healing process that would allow people to move on and work together as united communities rather than divided ones. However, some people criticised the Commission and stated that it had failed to achieve reconciliation between the black and white communities. Some felt that they had not received justice when someone who had killed a family member was granted amnesty. Others felt that the proceedings only helped to remind them of the horrors that had taken place when they had been working hard to forget.

Oasis of Peace

Israel is a country in conflict where two very different nations, Israel and Palestine, are trying to occupy the same land. There is continual strife and frequent war as each claims areas of land as its own. This has led to many atrocities on both sides where people have lost their loved ones, homes, towns and villages.

'Oasis of Peace' is a village just outside Jerusalem where Jews and Palestinians have chosen to live together. Here they recognise their differences and accept each other for who they are. The schools are bilingual and multicultural so that they learn to speak each other's languages and become aware of each other's religions and cultures. There is an atmosphere of openness and tolerance in the schools that encourages the children to understand, accept and appreciate each other. The school is open to anyone in the area who wishes to have their children educated together with children of the other faith.

Get Active 2

The reconciliation work of the 'Oasis of Peace' village extends outside its community.

1 Complete some research on this work. Choose an internet search engine and type in **www.nswas.org**. Find out about one of the following:

▶ The School of Peace

▶ The Pluralistic Spiritual Centre

▶ Humanitarian aid.

2 Working in pairs prepare a two minute speech about the work that is carried out in this area. Deliver your speech to the class.

5.4 The Corrymeela community

THE CORRYMEELA COMMUNITY

Within Northern Ireland, just outside Ballycastle, there is a reconciliation centre called Corrymeela. It was founded in 1965 by Ray Davey as an **ecumenical** Christian community. When it first opened, its aim was to help individuals and communities from both sides of the divide who had suffered through violence in Northern Ireland. It provided a 'safe place' for people to come and talk about their experiences and hear the stories of others. Very often this was the first time that people had had the opportunity to talk to someone of a tradition different from their own.

Ray Davey was born in 1915 in Dummurry, Belfast. His father was a Presbyterian minister and when he was older Ray also became a minister. After the Second World War he became the chaplain at Queen's University Belfast where he created a centre for Christian students to live together as a community. The community ensured that they weren't cut off from the rest of university life and encouraged Christians and non-Christians alike to come to many of their events.

Ray felt that it was important for the students to visit other European countries and meet the people who lived there. The visits that had the most impact on them were those that they made to other Christian communities; Agapé in Italy, Taizé in France and Iona in Scotland. These communities taught that Christianity should be lived out in a practical way by helping those in need. The students began to realise that a centre was needed in Northern Ireland that would create a safe place for people to meet. Here people from different backgrounds and political beliefs could meet together and talk about the problems, pain and suffering that they were experiencing.

There were other people who were also interested in making this happen and they came from many different backgrounds – ministers, missionaries, housewives, traders, people from industry, education and social work. As a group they got together with the shared aim of working for peace and understanding within Northern Ireland. They looked for suitable premises where a community could be established in order to try and make their dream a reality. In 1965 they discovered that the Holiday Fellowship Centre near Ballycastle was for sale. It was bought by the community and Corrymeela was opened on 30 October 1965 with 200 people present.

Get Active 1

Imagine the Belfast Telegraph is running a competition for aspiring young writers to write an article on the Corrymeela community. In less than 300 words, write a brief article outlining the aims and objectives of the community and the work that it does.

As peace has been established in Northern Ireland and the political parties try to work together, the work of Corrymeela continues.

Today the Corrymeela community wishes to:

▶ be a Christian community of reconciliation following the way of the gospel
▶ be in positive relationship with people regardless of class, religious opinion or political conviction
▶ create safe spaces where people of diverse backgrounds can come and meet each other, where there is an atmosphere of trust and acceptance and where differences can be acknowledged, explored and accepted
▶ work to realise a society whose priorities are justice, mutual respect, the participation of all, concern for the vulnerable and the stranger, stewardship of resources, and care for creation.

www.corrymeela.org

Today, in order to meet these aims Corrymeela is involved in a wide variety of programmes. It works with communities that live at the interface areas, where Catholics and Protestants live close to each other but on opposite sides of the peace wall. Very often these people come together to forge cross-community relationships. Corrymeela can organise training and workshops to give them the confidence to initiate their own programmes. They also assist groups in setting up projects which meet the needs of prisoners, both loyalist and republican, ex-prisoners and their families. They run 'faith and life' programmes that allow people to explore their faith with others from different traditions. There are many programmes that bring families together to help them move towards reconciliation, respect and trust. Finally they are involved in schools and run an extensive youth programme.

Corrymeela now has 150 members and over 5000 friends and supporters throughout the world. Each year over 6000 people take part in programmes at the Corrymeela Ballycastle Centre which has facilities for over 100 residents.

Get Active 2

Create a leaflet that informs people about the work of the Corrymeela community and makes them aware of the Corrymeela community website **www.corrymeela.org**.

Summary

▶ Sectarianism is a prejudice based on religious differences. This can be between different religions or between subdivisions within a religion. It can lead to violence and death.

▶ Reconciliation is the process of bringing differing groups together to enable them to understand more about each other and how to live together in peace.

Sectarianism and reconciliation: the big task

Now you have completed this chapter on 'Sectarianism and reconciliation', do the following task:

1   Write a letter inviting some local ministers and priests to come to your class to discuss the issues you have studied in this chapter.

2   Working in groups prepare questions for the visitors. As a class decide which questions you will ask in the time you have and who will be the spokesperson for each question.

3   Following the visit write a short account of what you have learnt from the question and answer session.

Chapter 6
Buddhism

Learning intentions

I am learning:

▶ to appreciate the historical Buddha and his teachings

▶ to examine the main groups within Buddhism and one of their leaders

▶ to explore the many different symbols within Buddhism and their meaning

▶ to understand Buddhist worship and festivals

▶ to discover the role of the Sangha within the Buddhist faith and community.

In your notebook complete the following task:

▶ Write down three things that make you happy.

▶ Write down one occasion when you felt really happy.

▶ How would you describe happiness?

▶ Write down three things that make you unhappy.

▶ Write down one occasion when you felt really unhappy.

▶ How would you describe unhappiness?

Everyone in our world will experience unhappiness and some more than others. This leads people to suffer and one of the major questions that Buddhism tries to answer is 'why do people suffer?' Within this chapter you will learn and understand the answer that Buddhism gives.

The Great Buddha of Kamakura, Kotokuin Temple, Japan

6.1 How it all began

The religion of Buddhism was founded in the fifth century BCE. The founder of the religion was a prince who lived in Lumbini (now located in Southern Nepal). This is his story:

1 Prince Siddhartha was born around 563 BCE in India. His father made sure that as he grew up he never saw suffering. He married and had a child.

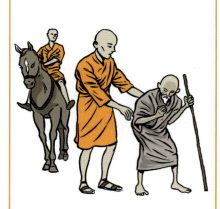

2 Whenever he wanted to leave the palace the King made sure that he would not encounter suffering – servants rode ahead to clear the road of poor, old and sick people.

3 One day he left with is servant Channa without telling his father and he saw four things that shocked him.

4 He saw an old man leaning on a stick. Channa explained that everyone gets old.

5 Next he saw a sick man covered in sores lying on the ground. Channa said the man was sick and that everyone experiences illness at some time in their lives.

6 Later he saw a funeral. Channa explained that people don't live forever. Everyone dies.

7 Finally he saw a holy man who looked peaceful and happy. Siddhartha wondered how anyone could be happy surrounded by old age, sickness and death. Channa said some people chose this life to help them understand suffering.

8 Siddhartha realised that all the luxury in the world would not make him happy unless he knew why people suffered? He had a major decision to make. He had to leave the palace to find the answer to his question.

9 Siddhartha joined some holy men and ate only a little food. He became so thin that you could see his spine through his stomach. Fasting, starving his body of food, didn't help Siddhartha find the answers to his questions.

10 Siddhartha left the holy men and travelled for several years continuing his search. He sat under a bodhi tree and meditated. During this meditation he discovered the answer to his question 'Why do people suffer?'. He received **enlightenment** and became the Buddha (which means 'enlightened' one).

11 The way to be happy, Siddhartha now believed, was to stop wanting things, to stop believing things last forever and to stop being selfish.

12 Siddhartha spent the rest of his life travelling and teaching others about how to become enlightened.

Buddhists believe that the Buddha's teaching answers the question about suffering and that the guidelines set down by him enable people to live their lives free from suffering. By following the guidelines people can achieve enlightenment and reach **Nirvana**. Unlike other religions Buddhists do not believe there is a god in charge of the world and everyone in it.

Get Active 1

Working in groups write and perform a role play for the rest of the class outlining the main events in the life of the Buddha. Remember to include all the information about why the Buddha left the palace and how he received enlightenment.

6.2 Buddhist beliefs 1

After his enlightenment the Buddha began to teach what he believed to others. His teachings can be split up into three areas:

▶ The Three Universal Truths

▶ The Four Noble Truths

▶ The Noble Eightfold Path

After his enlightenment, the Buddha was reluctant to teach the **Dhamma** to others. It was his compassion (**Karuna**) that motivated him to do it

The Three Universal Truths

ANICCA – nothing lasts forever and people, plants and the land are always changing every second, every minute, every day.

DUKKHA – life is unsatisfactory because it involves suffering. It includes things like being bored or uncomfortable and change. Nothing is completely perfect.

ANATTA – nothing is permanent and nothing lasts forever (even humans). They do not believe in a soul that goes from one body to another. What carries on to the next life is a 'life force' which the person has made in this life.

Like Hindus, Buddhists believe in **rebirth.** They believe that everyone lives many times. Buddhists believe that when a person dies he or she will be born again as a new person. Buddhists and Hindus call this cycle of birth, death and rebirth **Samsara.** The quality of your next life depends on your **Karma.** Karma is the combined effect of the good and bad deeds in your past lives. If people fully understand the Three Universal Truths then they can escape the cycle of birth, death and rebirth and enter Nirvana.

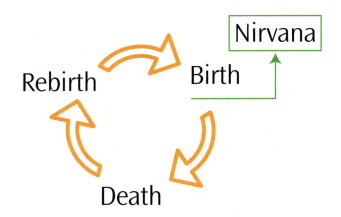

Get Active 1

1 In your notebook write the heading 'What do Buddhists believe? The Three Universal Truths'.

2 Draw a large circle and divide it into three. Write the name of one of the Three Universal Truths in one section of the circle. Write the second of the Three Universal Truths in another section, and likewise with the third.

3 Under each name write about what it means. Colour and decorate the diagram that you have made with appropriate images.

4 In your own words explain the Buddhist belief in rebirth, Samsara and Karma. You could use the diagram on the previous page to help you explain the beliefs.

The Four Noble Truths

The Buddha taught that suffering, Dukkha, was everywhere in life. He believed that people suffer because of greed and selfishness. People are always striving to have more or clinging to the things that they do have, not wanting things to change. He said that people can live a life without suffering if they believe that things do not stay the same all the time and they stop striving to have more and more. In order to do this they should follow the guidelines set down in the Noble Eightfold Path. These beliefs are called the Four Noble Truths.

The Four Noble Truths are:

1 Dukkha (suffering) is everywhere, all the time.

2 Dukkha is caused by greed and selfishness.

3 Greed and selfishness can be ended.

4 The way to end greed and selfishness is to follow the Noble Eightfold Path.

Get Active 2

1 Working in groups look back at your list of what causes people to suffer. Discuss the Four Noble Truths in your group using the following questions:

a Do you think the Buddha was right when he said that suffering is everywhere?

b Looking at your list of what causes people to suffer do you agree with the Buddha that suffering is caused by greed and selfishness?

c Do you think people can really live a life without suffering?

Appoint someone as a scribe to write down the main points of your discussion and a spokesperson for your group.

2 Report back to the rest of the class.

6.3 Buddhist beliefs 2

The Buddha said that you cannot reach Nirvana by living a life of luxury and you cannot reach Nirvana by living a life of deliberate poverty and starvation. He had lived in both of these ways and they had not brought him happiness or freedom from suffering. He taught his followers that they should follow a **Middle Way**. He said that the Middle Way had eight parts and that to make it work you must follow all of them. This is why the Buddha's Middle Way is known as the Noble Eightfold Path.

The Noble Eightfold Path

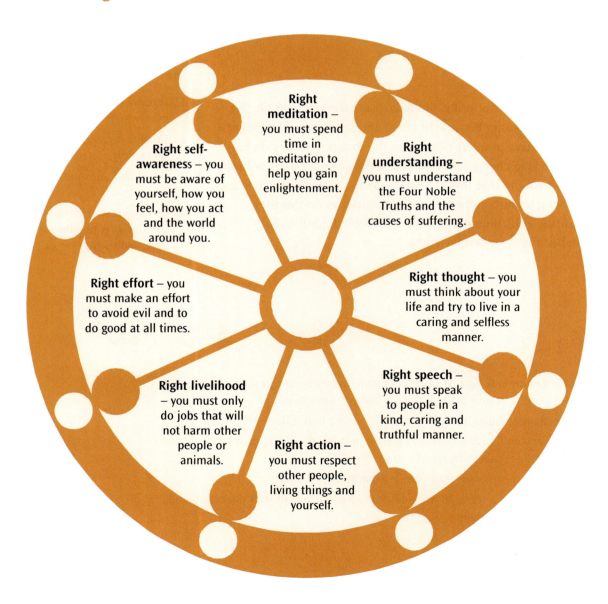

Right meditation – you must spend time in meditation to help you gain enlightenment.

Right self-awareness – you must be aware of yourself, how you feel, how you act and the world around you.

Right understanding – you must understand the Four Noble Truths and the causes of suffering.

Right effort – you must make an effort to avoid evil and to do good at all times.

Right thought – you must think about your life and try to live in a caring and selfless manner.

Right livelihood – you must only do jobs that will not harm other people or animals.

Right speech – you must speak to people in a kind, caring and truthful manner.

Right action – you must respect other people, living things and yourself.

Get Active 1

1   Write one or two sentences to explain what the Buddha meant by the 'Middle Way'.
2   Do you think that it would be difficult to follow the Eightfold Path? Give two reasons for your answer.
3   Would any of the steps be easier to follow? Explain why.
4   Which steps on the path would tell a Buddhist:
    a   to do his or her best not to call other people names?
    b   to be kind to animals?
    c   not to kill?
    d   not to drink alcohol or take drugs?

By following the guidelines set down in the Eightfold Path, Buddhists believe that they can achieve enlightenment, escape the cycle of rebirth and reach Nirvana. Buddhists say it is not possible to describe Nirvana. We do not know what Nirvana is like and we can only describe what it is *not* like. It is not life and it is not death. It is a state where there is no suffering, greed or anger. It is freedom from the cycle of death and rebirth. Buddhists believe that if they follow the Buddha's teachings well they will reach Nirvana. Reaching Nirvana is the goal of Buddhism.

Get Active 2

Imagine you are a practising Buddhist. A friend has just emailed you to ask about the main beliefs of your faith. Write a reply that explains:
    a   the Three Universal Truths
    b   the Four Noble Truths
    c   the Eightfold Path
    d   life after death
Ensure that you explain it as simply as possible.

6.4 Types of Buddhism

Although Buddhism has divided into different groups over the centuries, the fundamental teaching of the Buddha is the same for all these groups. The separate groups can be seen as different paths to reaching enlightenment.

Two main groups within Buddhism are Theravada and Mahayana.

Theravada Buddhism

Theravada Buddhism is strongest in Thailand, Cambodia, Laos and Sri Lanka and is sometimes called Southern Buddhism. The word Theravada means 'the way of the elders' and followers accept only the Pali Canon as their scriptures. The purpose of life is to reach Nirvana and not to be reborn again. However, this can only be achieved by living the life of a monk or nun and following a strict monastic code. Lay people (people who are not monks or nuns) can only hope that they will be reborn into a monastic life. They can help their chances of a good rebirth by helping monks and nuns throughout their lives.

Mahayana Buddhism

Mahayana Buddhism began in the first century CE and is strongest in Tibet, China and Korea and is sometimes called Northern Buddhism. Mahayana Buddhism is seen as more liberal and followers accept the Pali Canon and later writings in their scriptures (Tripitaka). They also believe in Boddhisatvas – people who have gained enlightenment but have continued with life on earth in order to teach others and help them to attain enlightenment. Anyone (not just monks and nuns) can achieve enlightenment within Mahayana Buddhism.

Get Active 1

1 Read the information above and make a list of three differences between Theravada and Mahayana Buddhism.
2 As a class split into two groups. Each group should research one of the main forms of Buddhism to find out more information about it. You could use class textbooks, the school library or the internet. Each person should find out two new facts to share with their group.
3 Working as a group write down the facts that you have found out on a large sheet of poster paper. Share this with the rest of the class.

The Dalai Lama

One of the most famous leaders within Buddhism is the Dalai Lama. He is the leader of Tibetan Buddhism which is closely associated with the Mahayana tradition. According to Tibetan belief the current Dalai Lama is the fourteenth rebirth of a past **lama** who decided to be reborn again in order to continue teaching. Within Tibetan Buddhism, choosing to be reborn is called tulku. As the leader of Tibet the Dalai Lama had to leave in 1959 after the occupation of Tibet by the Chinese. He has since lived in India and has set up a Tibetan community in Dharamsala, Northern India.

The Dalai Lama

Throughout his time in exile the Dalai Lama has spoken out about the Chinese occupation of Tibet and has been seeking a peaceful solution to the problem. He received the Nobel Peace Prize in 1989 and is seen as an important religious figure around the world.

Get Active 2

Look at the following quotations from the Dalai Lama:

All major religious traditions carry basically the same message; that is love, compassion and forgiveness. The important thing is they should be part of our daily lives.

It is necessary to help others, not only in our prayers, but in our daily lives. If we find we cannot help others, the least we can do is to desist from harming them.

Whether one believes in a religion or not and whether one believes in rebirth or not, there isn't anyone who doesn't appreciate kindness and compassion.

1 Work in groups of three. Each person chooses one of the quotations to write down in their notebook. Look back at your work on the teaching of the Buddha. Explain how the quotation links to the Noble Eightfold Path.
2 Share your work with the others in the group.
3 Create a Dalai Lama quotation board – write up the quotations and explain how they link to the teaching of the Buddha.

6.5 Buddhist symbols

Get Active 1

Choose one of the beliefs that you have studied about Buddhism so far and design a symbol that you think best represents it. Write a short paragraph explaining the symbol.

Dharmachakra

Buddhism contains many different symbols that represent Buddha and his teachings. During the early centuries of Buddhism, images of the historical Buddha were not permitted. The eight-spoke wheel was therefore developed to symbolise Buddha turning the wheel of truth and law. The wheel is one of the earliest and most important symbols in the Buddhist religion. It is called the Dharmachakra: dharma meaning teaching and truth, chakra meaning law and wheel. Every part of the wheel is symbolic. The eight 'spokes' represent the wisdom of the Eightfold Path set out by Buddha in his teachings. The 'hub' of the wheel symbolises the discipline required to follow the path. Finally, the 'rim' of the wheel represents the concentration that binds everything together. The wheel also illustrates the endless cycle of rebirth, which one can escape by following the teachings of Buddha.

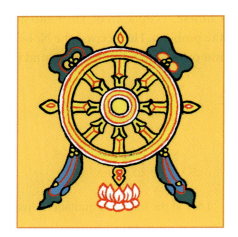

Lotus flower

The lotus flower is another ancient symbol of Buddhism. The mud at the bottom of the pond in which the flower begins represents the mind and how it is clouded with ignorance and selfishness. The path the flower follows through the water represents the journey the mind takes towards enlightenment. The flower blooming in the sunlight symbolises the enlightened mind.

The Eight Auspicious Symbols

The wheel and the lotus flower are considered two of the 'auspicious' symbols by most Buddhists. The remaining six are:

Parasol

Protection from suffering.

Golden fishes

No fear of drowning in suffering.

Treasure vase

Long life and prosperity.

Conch shell

The sound of the dharma reaching far and wide.

Endless knot

Everything in life is connected.

Victory banner

Victory over passion, fear of death, pride and lust.

Get Active 2

There are many more symbols in Buddhism. Using an internet search engine, type in 'Buddhist symbols' to find out what some of these are and create a poster. The poster should contain one symbol mentioned in this book and three others. Ensure that you have an illustration of the symbol along with a short explanation. The posters could be used to create a display in the classroom of Buddhist symbols.

Images of the Buddha

Although for several hundred years there were no images of the Buddha, nowadays there are many. He is usually depicted in one of three positions: Standing, sitting or lying down. Other characteristics that can often be found within these images include:

▶ long ear lobes representing honour

▶ a round mark on his forehead representing a third eye, indicating that he can see and know things that ordinary people cannot

▶ curly hair representing a holy man.

The position of his hands is also important and indicates an element of enlightenment. The hand positions are called 'mudras'.

The three positions the Buddha is usually depicted in – lying down, sitting and standing

Mudras

A mudra is a ritual or symbolic gesture usually made with the hands. Most of the images of the Buddha have the hands in a mudra position. Six of the main positions are shown below:

MEDITATION

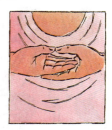

The hand position of meditation.

TEACHING

Teaching the dharma.

ENLIGHTENMENT

Calling the earth to witness the truth of his words.

PREACHING

Turning the wheel of the law.

CHARITY

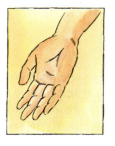

This represents charity.

REASSURANCE

Blessing and protection. Do not fear.

6.6 Worship

It may seem strange that Buddhists take part in worship given that they don't believe in a god or gods controlling everything. However, for a Buddhist, worship is about showing gratitude and respect to the historical Buddha. It also helps to remind them of the teachings of Buddhism and to reflect upon how they are practising it. It is something to feel and enjoy either by themselves or with others. There are no rules in Buddhism about how often a person should worship and each form of Buddhism will have a different approach. The word used to describe worship is 'puja', and this normally takes place at a shrine. Shrines can be in someone's home or within a temple.

Buddhist shrine, Belfast

Shrines

There are many different types of shrine ranging from quite simplistic to more elaborate. However, each of them will contain the same following key elements:

▶ Images of the Buddha: There will be at least one image of the Buddha, representing enlightenment. This will be the central focus of the shrine.

▶ Seven offering bowls: Offerings are made as if the Buddha himself were there. To offer him water is a sign of respect and reverence. Food may also be offered.

▶ Flowers: Flowers are beautiful but they will wither and die. They represent the impermanence of life.

▶ Candles: These represent the wisdom of Buddha lighting up the world.

▶ Incense: As the aroma fills the room it represents the dharma spreading around the world.

Meditation

Meditation is an important part of Buddhist worship. It is a technique that is used to help reach enlightenment. Meditation is a way to quieten a busy mind. A simple meditation will focus on one thing, for example, breathing. The person will concentrate upon the process of breathing – the air filling the lungs and flowing out of the nostrils. Through doing this, calmness and an awareness of oneself is developed.

Get Active 1

1 Sit with your feet flat on the floor and your back straight against a chair. Place your hands in the meditation position on your lap. Close your eyes.

2 Breathe slowly in and out. Become aware of your breathing as the air fills your lungs and leaves through your nostrils. Silently count 'one'. Take another breath and count 'two'. Continue to do this until you have reached ten. If your mind wanders at any point focus on your breathing and start again from 'one'.

3 Discuss with the class how this made you feel.

Mandala

Within some traditions meditation can be done through an activity. As long as the mind is totally focused on one thing this can lead to a feeling of calmness. Some monks will create beautiful patterns out of sand which can take hours or even days to complete. However, when they are finished they will be swept away. These patterns are called **mandalas** and it is believed that it is the process of creating them that is important and not the end product. Buddhists believe that they shouldn't cling on to anything – even beautiful patterns that they have created.

A Buddhist monk completing a mandala

Mantras

Another popular tradition in meditation is to use sounds and words. These are known as **mantras** and are believed to have spiritual power if continually repeated. Each mantra invokes an aspect of enlightenment. Some Buddhists believe that through repeating the mantra over and over this aspect of enlightenment will break through into their minds. The most famous mantra comes from the Tibetan tradition and is **Om Mani Padme Hum**. This is a mantra that expresses love and compassion for all. Mantras are very difficult to translate as it is the sounds that are significant and not their meaning.

Prayer wheels and flags

Prayer wheels and flags are part of Tibetan worship and are used to spread spiritual blessings and well being. Within a prayer wheel the mantra 'Om Mani Padme Hum' is printed many times onto paper and also on to the outer covering. The turning of the wheel is considered the same as speaking the mantra. If the mantra is copied 100 times then one turn of the wheel means that it has been spoken 100 times. This releases the power of the mantra upon the community.

Tibetan Buddhists believe that the power of the mantra can be carried on the wind. They therefore often copy mantras onto flags. The flags are usually five different colours: blue, white, red, green and yellow. The colour of the flags is significant as they represent the five elements (wind, air, earth, fire and water), the five directions (north, south, east, west and centre) and the five wisdoms (compassion, harmony, wisdom of sight, kindness and perfect wisdom).

Get Active 2

Create a Tibetan prayer flag. Using an internet search engine, research Tibetan mantras. Choose a mantra and on a piece of coloured paper (either blue, white, red, green or yellow) write out the mantra. String the flags together and display them in the classroom.

Stupas

Stupas are religious monuments which traditionally contained the remains of the Buddha or one of the great Buddhist teachers. Early stupas were simple mounds of earth that covered up these religious relics and because of this they became places of pilgrimage and worship. Over time stupas have evolved and are now sometimes referred to as 'spiritual monuments'.

The symbolism of a stupa is complex and each component represents something different. One symbolism of the stupa is the Buddha crowned and sitting in the meditation position on a lion throne.

Shewdagon Pagoda, a stupa in Burma

Buddhist scripture

There are a vast number of **scriptures** and religious texts in Buddhism but not one universal book that is used by all. The scriptures can be roughly divided into two sections. Firstly, the words spoken by the Buddha and secondly commentaries, collections of quotes and histories. The earliest collection of Buddhist teachings is called the **Tripitaka**. This is also known as the three baskets as it is divided into three sections. In the Theravada tradition these are the only scriptures recognised as the words of the Buddha. The Mahayana tradition reveres the Tripitaka as a sacred text but adds to it the **sutras**. These are a collection of teachings which contain distinctive Mahayana ideas.

For some Buddhists, studying the scriptures is an important form of worship as this is how they learn about their religion. Some Buddhists will chant the scriptures during worship and others will not read any at all.

Get Active 3

Imagine you are a Tibetan monk or nun and you have been asked to write an article for the local religious magazine about how you worship. Within your article include all the different aspects mentioned in this section explaining how, when and why worship is done. More information about Tibetan worship can be found on the internet or in a library.

6.7 Festivals

There are many Buddhist festivals and each tradition has its own that they celebrate but there are some that are common to all. Festivals are always happy times full of enjoyment. The importance of festivals is that they are a time for Buddhists to come together and celebrate in an atmosphere of fun and fellowship. What happens during a festival is not significant but the attitude of the people taking part is. During festivals there are always opportunities to learn more about Buddha and his teachings.

Buddhist monks line up to receive alms at the Marble Temple Wat Benchamabophet in Bangkok Thailand

Wesak

The most important Buddhist festival is called Wesak. This is celebrated in May during the full moon. It celebrates the birth, enlightenment and death of Buddha and is also known as Buddha Day. It is during this time that Buddhists reflect upon how they might gain enlightenment. In order to prepare for the festival homes are cleaned and special Wesak lanterns are made. People will go to the temples to worship and make offerings of food, candles and flowers to the monks.

New Year

New Year is an important festival for Buddhists and is celebrated at different times by the various Buddhist traditions. In Thailand it takes place in April and is called Songkran Day. During Songkran Day images of the Buddha are washed and people splash water on each other. Water is a symbol of cleansing, refreshment and new life. Fish and eels are also released into rivers and caged birds are freed. This is to show the love and compassion of the Buddha. The festival lasts for three days and people spend time playing games, flying kites, dancing and performing traditional plays. The festival ends with worship in the temple.

Within some of the Buddhist traditions every full moon is important and is celebrated with a festival. At the July full moon many traditions celebrate the time when the Buddha started to teach the dharma.

Get Active 1

1   Working in groups, choose one of the Buddhist traditions and research the festivals that they celebrate.

2   Prepare a one minute talk on one of these festivals. Ensure that it isn't one that has already been mentioned in this book. Describe to the class which tradition it is from, the name of the festival, what it celebrates and why.

6.8 The Sangha

Sangha means community and is one of the 'three jewels' that makes up Buddhism, the Buddha and the dharma being the other two. The Sangha can be the monastic element of Buddhism or the Buddhist community that encompasses all the members including monks and nuns.

The first monastic Sangha was established by the Buddha himself with the aim of ensuring that his teachings were passed on. Discipline was reinforced and an example of how to live the Buddhist life was available to the rest of the community. Today the monastic Sangha is governed by a set of rules found in the **vinaya** which was originally passed on orally by the Buddha to his disciples. As Buddhism spread each tradition developed its own vinaya with rules and punishments.

Buddhist community, Belfast

When a monk enters the Sangha he takes vows and is expected to obey all the rules. There are approximately 225 rules but this varies within the traditions. Once these vows have been taken they can be 'given back' so that the person can leave the monastic lifestyle. This can be done up to three times within their life.

Monks and nuns wear special robes and in many traditions their heads are shaved. Each tradition has its own rules and some monastic communities only have one meal a day which must be eaten before midday. The food is often provided for them by the local community who believe that they gain merit by providing for the monks. The role of the monastic Sangha hasn't changed since the Buddha established the first one. It is the monks and nuns role to pass on the Buddha's teachings and live by his disciplines and set an example to all.

The community Sangha is the fellowship of believers. This is important as it allows people to come together and explore the Buddhist teachings. It is difficult to live a Buddhist lifestyle by yourself so the community helps to support and encourage you on your journey to enlightenment.

Get Active 1

Using an internet search engine find out what a typical day for a Buddhist monk or nun consists of. Write a timetable that outlines the activities of the day.

Summary

▶ Prince Siddhartha experienced luxury and hardship but neither of them brought him happiness. He believed that suffering occurred because people wanted things. Suffering also occurred when people found it difficult to accept that people and objects change.

▶ There are three main sets of beliefs within Buddhism:
1 the Three Universal Truths
2 the Four Noble Truths
3 the Noble Eightfold Path.

▶ While there are many different sects within Buddhism, the two main traditions are the Theravada and the Mahayana.

▶ Symbols are very important within Buddhism.

▶ Although Buddhists don't worship any gods, worship is still important within their faith.

▶ There are many festivals within Buddhism. However, the most important is Wesak or Buddha Day.

Buddhism: the big task

Working in groups, give a presentation on Buddhism to your class.

Before you begin decide with your teacher what the success criteria for the presentation will be.

When each group gives their presentation every pupil will give it a mark out of ten. The mark must relate to the success criteria and whether the group has completed them all. When all presentations have been given the teacher will collect the marks, add them together and give a prize to the group with the highest score.

In your groups decide which method of presentation you are going to use.

You must include the following in your presentation:

1 how Buddhism began
2 the main beliefs
3 symbols within Buddhism
4 buddhist worship
5 festivals
6 the Sangha.

Glossary

A

abolitionist – a person who campaigned for the end of slavery and the slave trade

addicted – a psychological or physical dependence on a substance

agnostic – someone who doesn't know if there is a God or not

amnesty – a general pardon for offences

apartheid – a political system in South Africa from 1948 to the early 1990s that separated black people from white people and gave privileges to white people

atheist – someone who believes that there is no God

auspicious – the favoured signs and symbols within Buddhism

B

bonded labour – being forced to work to pay off a debt

boycott – refusal to deal with a given organisation

C

campesinos – Spanish word for poor farmers in Central America

civil rights movement – citizens trying to achieve equal rights for all within a society

D

DNA – the main component of the chromosomes of all living things

Dhamma – this is the collective word for the teaching of the Buddha and includes: The Three Universal Truths, The Four Noble Truths and The Noble Eightfold Path

dharmachakra – the name given to the symbolic wheel within Buddhism

E

ecumenical – different Christian churches working together for unity

embryo – an unborn baby in the early stages of development

enlightenment – to fully understand a concept, theory or philosophy

F

fetus – an unborn baby in the later stages of development

free will – the ability to choose how to act, whether rightly or wrongly

G

genetically engineered – alteration of the genetic structure of an organism for a particular purpose

J

just war – a war fought that is conducted within a legal and moral framework

K

Karma – the Buddhist belief that our actions in this life will have an effect on our future life through rebirth

Karuna – this is compassion. The Buddha showed Karuna by sharing his teachings with others

L

lama – the title given to a spiritual leader within Tibetan Buddhism

Love Ethic – situation ethics is described as the love ethic because the key principle is that we should make decisions based on love

M

mandalas – beautiful patterns created to aid meditation

mantra – a commonly repeated word or phrase chanted or sung as an incantation or prayer

martyr – a person who willingly suffers death rather than renounce his or her religion

meditations – continued or extended thought; reflection; contemplation

Middle Way – the Buddhist Noble Eightfold Path: guidelines on how to live life

ministry – the act of serving

moral evil – when a person does evil of their own free will

morals – concerned with right and wrong conduct; based on a sense of right and wrong

moral dilemma – a difficult decision that has be to made based on the right and wrong action

moral values – the guidelines/rules that help people make moral decisions

mudra – symbolic gesture within Buddhism – usually made with the hands

mystical – something which has spiritual significance which is beyond human understanding

N

natural evil – an evil event not caused by a person

Glossary

Nirvana – Buddhist belief – freedom from the endless cycle of personal reincarnations, with their consequent suffering. A state of peace that is achieved when suffering and its causes are overcome.

Noble Eightfold Path – eight rules that guide Buddhists throughout their lives

O

Om Mani Padme Hum – a popular mantra within the Buddhist tradition

omnipotent – unlimited power

omnipresent – present everywhere

omniscient – all-knowing

oppression – to be controlled by cruelty or force

P

placenta – carries nourishment from the mother's blood to the embryo or fetus

principle of love – the central theme of situation ethics: that everyone should base their decisions on love for others

R

rebirth – a renewed existence, activity, or growth

reconciliation – to bring into agreement or harmony

Reformation – the religious movement in the sixteenth century that reformed the Roman Catholic Church and that led to the establishment of Protestant churches

S

Samsara – Buddhist belief in the cycle of birth, death and rebirth

Sangha – the name given to the Buddhist community

saviour sibling – a child created to save the live of a brother or sister

scriptures – religious writings

sectarianism – prejudice based on religious differences

segregation – to separate or set apart from others or from the majority

social reformer – a person who campaigns to change society and improve people's way of life

situation ethics – a system of making decisions developed by Joseph Fletcher based on Jesus' commandment 'Love your neighbour as yourself'

stupas – a monumental pile of earth or other material, in memory of the Buddha or a Buddhist saint, and commemorating some event or marking a sacred spot

sutras – a collection of teachings from the Buddha

T

temperance movement – attempt to reduce the amount of alcohol consumed within a community or society in general, and even to prohibit its production and consumption entirely

theist – someone who believes that there is a God

theologian – someone who studies the nature of God and religious truth; they use rational inquiry into religious questions

Tripitaka – a collection of Buddhist scriptures

tithing – a religious tax: giving a percentage of your income to God

U

utilitarianism – conduct should be directed towards promoting the greatest happiness of the greatest number of people

V

vinaya – a set of rules by which the Sangha is governed

vocation – the belief that God has called you to do a particular job

W

wesek – Buddhist festival that celebrates the birth, enlightenment and death of Buddha. It is also known as Buddha Day

Index

Index